©2013 by Design Media Publishing Limited
This edition published in February 2013

Design Media Publishing Limited
20/F Manulife Tower
169 Electric Rd, North Point
Hong Kong
Tel: 00852-28672587
Fax: 00852-25050411
E-mail: suisusie@gmail.com
www.designmediahk.com

Editing: QIN Li
Editorial Assistant: Helen Liu
Translator: Katy Lee
Proofreading: Catherine Chang
Design/Layout: YANG Chunling

ISBN 978-988-15662-6-3

Printed in China

SCHOOL BUILDINGS

Edited by QIN Li   Translated by Katy Lee

DESIGN MEDIA PUBLISHING LIMITED

FOREWORD

In the recent ten years in China, with the nationwide strategy of "invigorating the country through science, technology and education", the implementation of compulsory education, and the rapid development of economy, educational architecture including universities, colleges, middle schools and primary schools has been growing at an unprecedented pace. Such fast development of educational architecture is rare in China and even in the world, in terms of both construction scale and speed. Thanks to the enthusiastic construction, school facilities are greatly improved for better educational environments, and architects get more opportunities to produce good architecture.

Many of the recently-completed school buildings are designed with innovative concepts. Generally speaking, nowadays when land resources become increasingly limited and construction sites grow larger and larger, architecture integration has become a trend, especially in educational contexts. In many schools and campuses, integrated complexes have been built with vertical and horizontal organisation of spaces to achieve a high efficiency in space utilisation. Various programmes are densely organised. Furthermore, new spaces that are rarely seen in traditional schools are added, such as lounges, restaurants, gathering and activity spaces. In this way, not only land resources are better utilised, but also school space becomes much more diversified and school life more interesting and lively.

From the perspective of architectural design, in the educational architecture built in recent years, compared with those built before the policy of "reform and opening-up", architects paid more attention to breaking up conventions in school design. School buildings used to have isolated and closed spaces, but now architects would like to build open spaces to stimulate interactive teaching, with more spaces for sharing and communication among students and teachers. Undoubtedly, the most attractive thing in school life for students is various activities. Therefore, architects should spare no effort in creating satisfying activity spaces, which not only are important for students to enjoy a diversified and interesting school life, but also give unique identity to a school.

While architects have reached an agreement on the significance of diversity and identity for educational architecture, however, we still observed the stereotypes of school building recurring. Simple replication of conventional school architecture still happens, and on the contrary, some schools go to extremes in seeking magnificent architecture regardless of cost. They prefer rigid axes, large plazas and luxurious appearances. Actually, we believe school spaces should be humanistic, and full of vigour instead of magnificence or luxury. In school architecture we should pay attention to culture rather than dignity or authority. School buildings should set good examples in being resource-saving and avoid fervent craving for greatness in building scale or appearance.

By contrast, many middle and primary schools in remote areas as well as hope schools in poverty-stricken areas have set good examples for educational architecture. Local materials and techniques are applied to reduce cost. Modern design approaches and traditional construction skills are perfectly combined, producing new unique contemporary school buildings. In these buildings we find that teaching and learning spaces can be quite interesting, and even fascinating! Thus we foresee a promising future for educational architecture in China, which would be full of joy, diversity, and vitality.

QIN Li
July 10th, 2012

CONTENTS

CHINA ACADEMY OF ART, XIANGSHAN CAMPUS
Hangzhou, Zhejiang Province
WANG Shu, LU Wenyu/The Amateur Architecture Studio, Contemporary Architecture Creation Study Centre, China Academy of Art

Gross Floor Area: Phase I Project 70,000m², Phase II Project 78,000m²
Design/Completion Time: Phase I Project 2001/2004,
Phase II Project 2004/2007
Architect: WANG Shu & LU Wenyu / The Amateur Architecture Studio &
Contemporary Architecture Creation Study Centre, China Academy of Art
Photographer: LV Hengzhong
Client: China Academy of Art

The new campus of China Academy of Art is located around Xiangshan Mountain, Hangzhou. The master plan of its phase I project is a morphological simulation of the natural relationships between mountains. Ten building units imply the trend of the mountains, which is obviously in association with the former villages on the site. Phase I project, which was designed in 2001 and completed in 2004, is occupied by the Public Art Institute, the Media and Animation Institute, library and gymnasium.

The Xiangshan Campus, which is generally in a mixed pattern of traditional academy and learning garden, embraces various styles of structure: the cloister like the one in an abbey gleaming behind the window on the lofty fir-slab wall, a combination structure of the Renaissance master's workshop and the modern studio, Bauhaus's workshop, as the symbol of elementary education on modern art, structured as an enclosed pedestal for all building units, and even the scattered and disordered site like the practice ground in Buddhist Cave Temples. All of this, finally joined in the recall and emotion of changeable landscape, displays the parallel gesture to the landscape around. The concealed bearing of the site shows the vivid declaration of the campus education quality and survival environment. The building in the site trends to hide itself, as a metaphor which the art education hiding behind the landscape after contributing itself.

The Xiangshan Phase I project is partitioned by courtyards with openings facing the mountain in different angles and the site where it locates. The angles, openings and locations are precisely defined. Based on the partition, the form and the detail of the units are made accordingly to interpret the relationship between the site and the scene. The phase II project at the south of the Xiangshan hill was designed in 2004 and completed in 2007, which consists of ten large buildings and two small ones. It contains the School of Architectural Art, the School of Design, art gallery, gymnasium,

students' residential building and dining hall. The new buildings are all arranged at the margin of the ground, which is in the same direction as the hill stretches and similar with the local traditional buildings. Between the buildings and the hill, a large space is vacated, in which the original farm, river and pound are preserved. The form of each architecture changes naturally along with the undulation of Xiangshan hill.

In the campus, the building plans look like something arranged by accident; space feels like vacant or compact, public or private; two elevations may be far from each other in one building; all of this compose a series of locations which are waiting for some events to happen quickly. There is no strict structure, but the real life will be easily live here. This is the understanding to the traditional Chinese garden, which is especially expressed in the phase II project at the south of Xiangshan. The same as phase I project, the land beside which buildings and roads stand is released to the farmers, to plant crops. Land tax will not be charged. A 200-metre-long water channel connects the river and runs across the campus, which is not only regarded as a landscape, but also supplies the field and the pond with water.

The architectural structure consists of concrete with steel-bar frame, steel in some parts, and brick walls, which are common in local area. By using a lot of low-cost recycled bricks and tiles, and taking full advantage of local handcraft construction, the local masonry of multi-size bricks and the modern architectural technique are integrated, which creates a thick wall system that is thermally insulated. Besides, it not only saves the resources, but also makes great impact on the ecological consciousness of teachers and students. Like the phase I, the phase II project at the south of Xiangshan, takes a period of 14 months, when The Amateur Architecture Studio are working in the process. Many problems, which come from the handwork during construction process, were solved by working at the location.

1

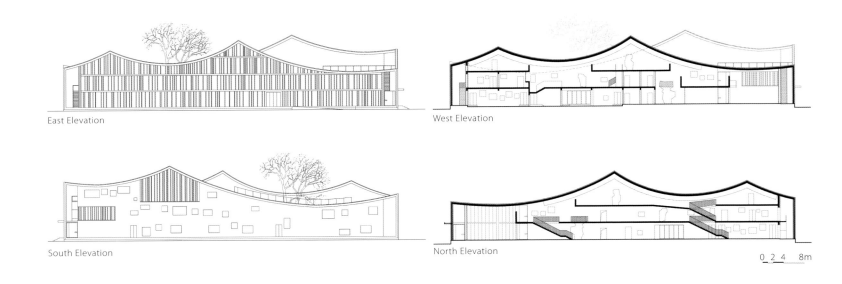

East Elevation

West Elevation

South Elevation

North Elevation

0 2 4 8m

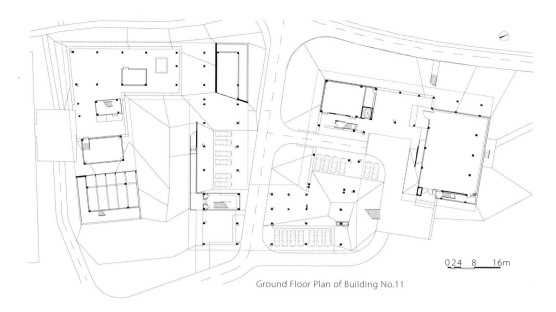

Ground Floor Plan of Building No.11

0 2 4 8   16m

3

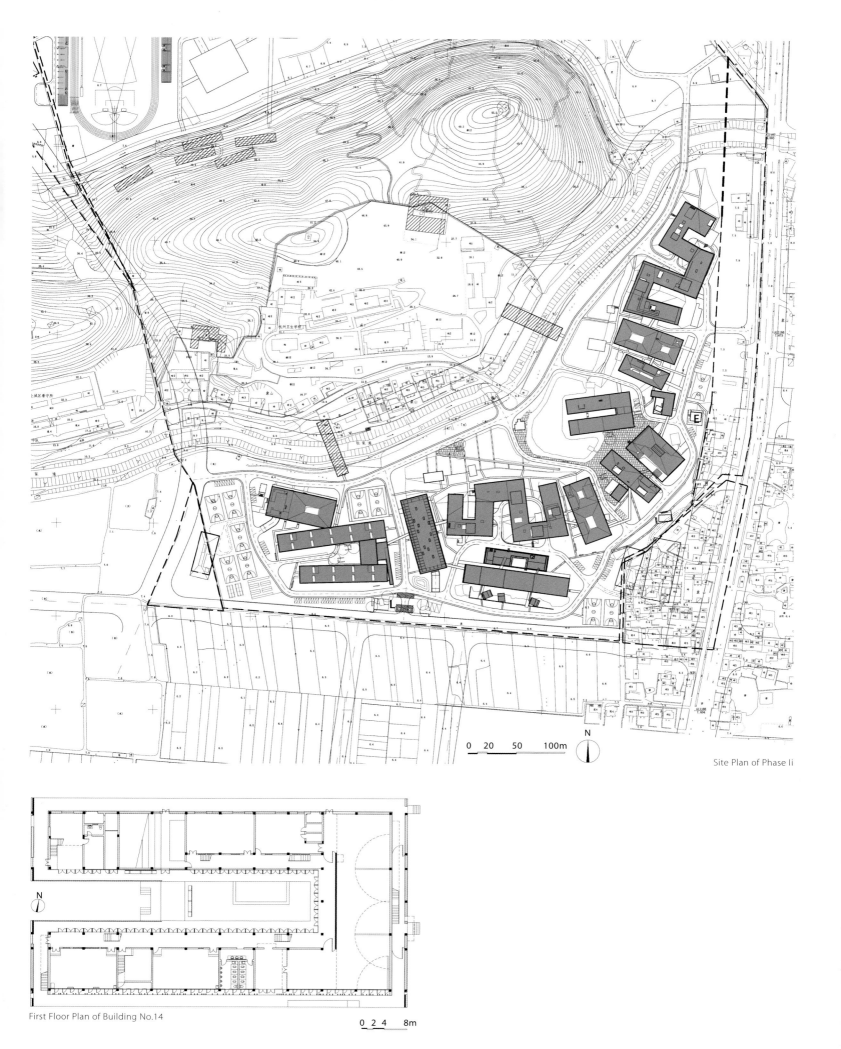

Site Plan of Phase Ii

First Floor Plan of Building No.14

0 2 4   8m

013

4

4. Roof view of Building No. 21
5. Interior view of Building No. 21

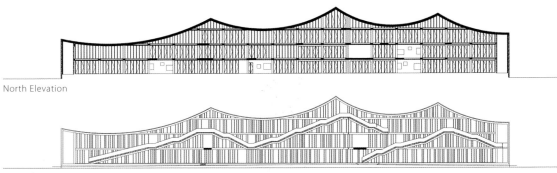

North Elevation

South Elevation

6

6. Bird's-eye view of Building No.19 from the north

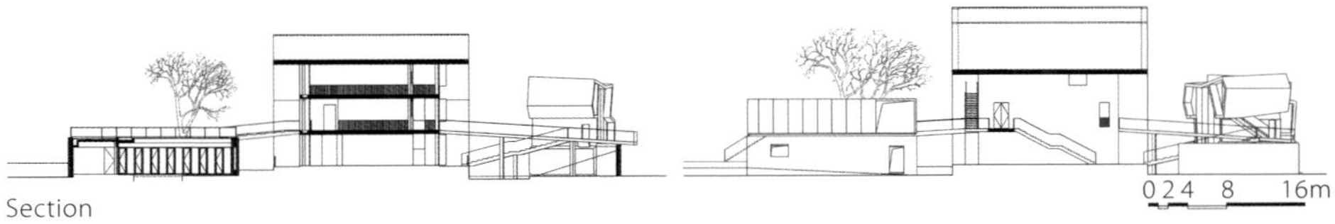

Section

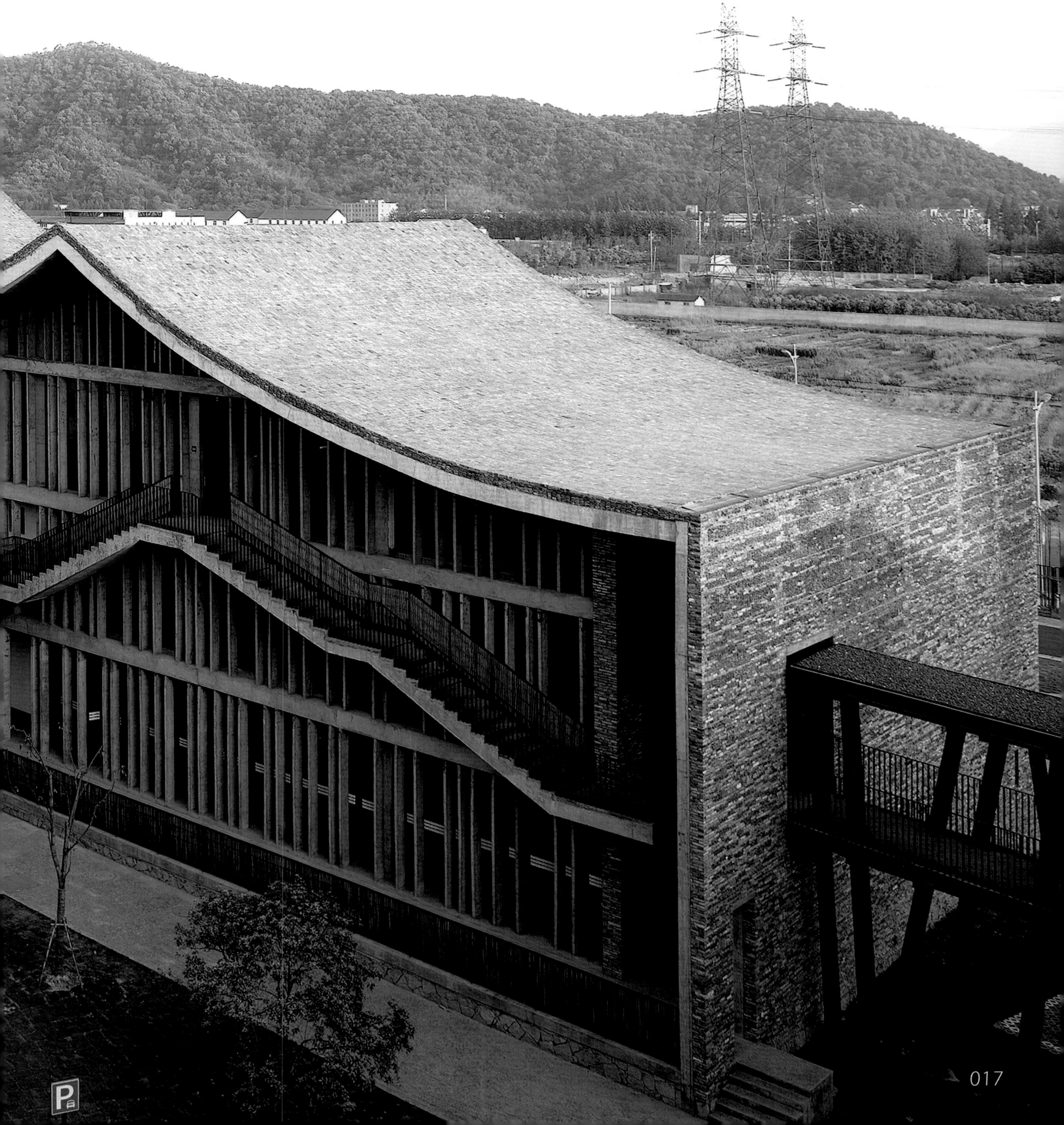

7. Courtyard view of Building No.12

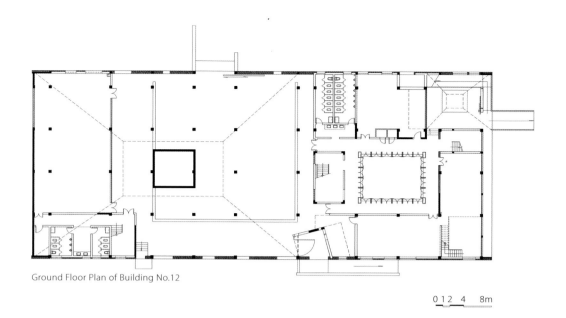

Ground Floor Plan of Building No.12

0 1 2　4　　8m

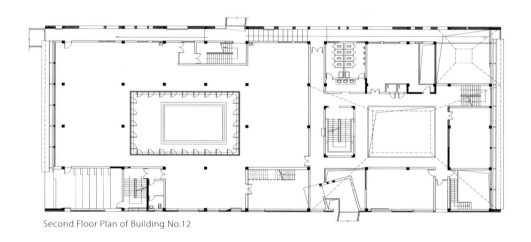

Second Floor Plan of Building No.12

N

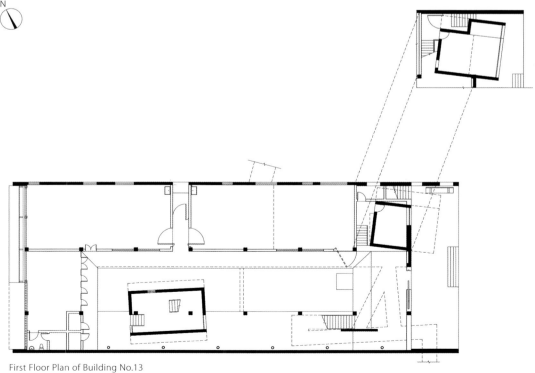

First Floor Plan of Building No.13

0 1 2　4　　8m

8. Overview of Building No.11

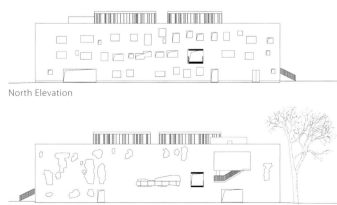

North Elevation

South Elevation

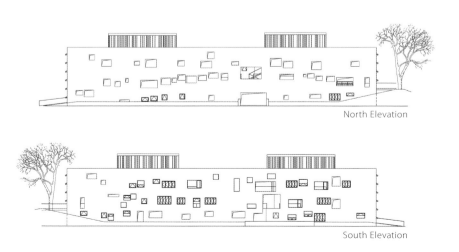

North Elevation

South Elevation

9. West view of Building No.11

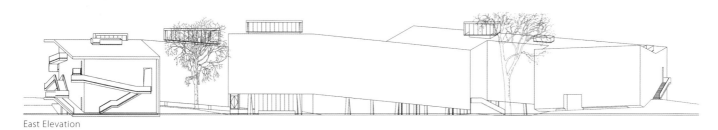

East Elevation

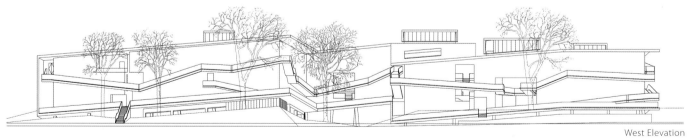

West Elevation

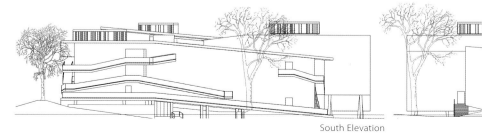

South Elevation

North Elevation

10. Corridor inside Building No.11
11. Half-open classroom
12. Exterior view of Building No.13

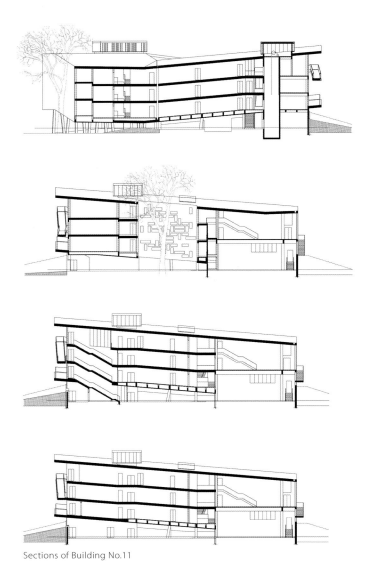

Sections of Building No.11

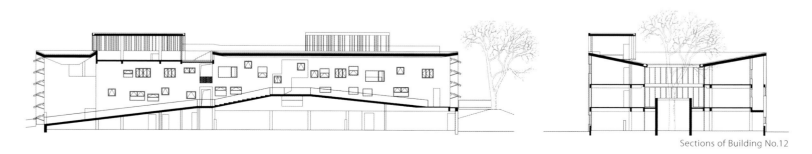

Sections of Building No.12

13

13. Northwest view of Building No.15 at night
14. Courtyard of building No.13
15. Staircase of building No.13

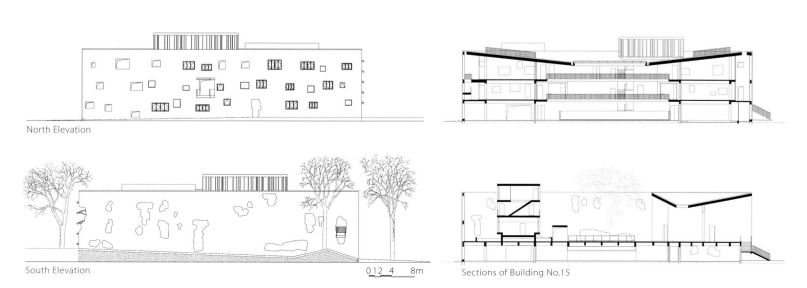

North Elevation

South Elevation

0 1 2 4   8m

Sections of Building No.15

14

15

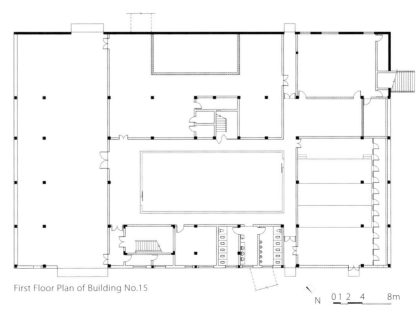

First Floor Plan of Building No.15

N 0 1 2 4   8m

JISHOU UNIVERSITY RESEARCH AND EDUCATION BUILDING AND HUANG YONG YU MUSEUM
Jishou, Hunan
Yung Ho CHANG / Atelier FCJZ

Gross Floor Area: 25,727.2m²
Jishou University Research and Education Building: 22,032.9m²
Huang Yongyu Museum: 3,688.3m²
Design/Completion Time: 2003-2004/2006
Principal Architect: Yung Ho CHANG / Atelier FCJZ
Project Architect: CHEN Long
Design Team: HU Xian, ZHANG Bo, HE Huishan, NI Jianhui
Collaborator: Yishe Architectural Design Consultants Co., Ltd., Beijing
Client: Jishou University

The project is located at the campus of Jishou University in Jishou City, Hunan Province, and is mainly concerned with two important issues relating to site: one is the relationship between architecture and its surrounding environment, and the other is how to establish relationships with local architectural tradition and culture.

The entire campus of the University was built on a hilly area, and nearly all the buildings were built against the hill. The site of the project sits on the south of the artificial lake at the campus centre, where it was formerly a slope which was later terraced. The Research Education Building and the Museum form a wedge-shaped composite section that inserts itself into the land. The building mass, multiple roofs and integrated windows blur the vertical and horizontal forms of walls and roofs, which in turn contributed to rebuilding and reestablishing the physical presence of the site.

Respect for local architectural culture has been developed into two types in Jishou: one is the preservation of "specimen buildings" in the old town, and the other is the duplication of local single residence regardless of structure, material, function, scale, etc. of the new building. Under such circumstances, the architects conformed to contemporary architectural conventions, and decided to keep the immense volume. They tried to bring the pattern of local residential groups into the new building, visually establishing a relationship between the new architecture and local architectural culture. Therefore, conceptually the architecture is both a "hill" and a "village".

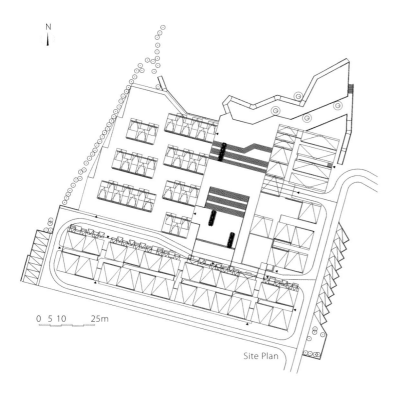

N

0 5 10   25m

Site Plan

1. Passageway on the seventh
   floor of Academic Building
2. Bird's eye view
3. Entrance plaza

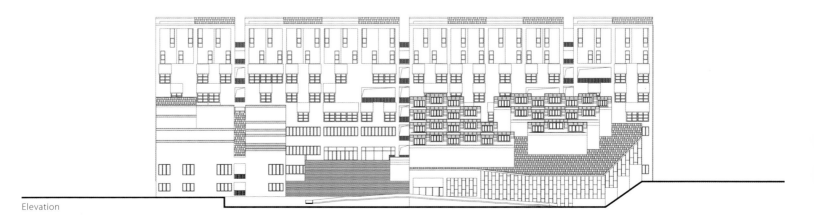

Elevation

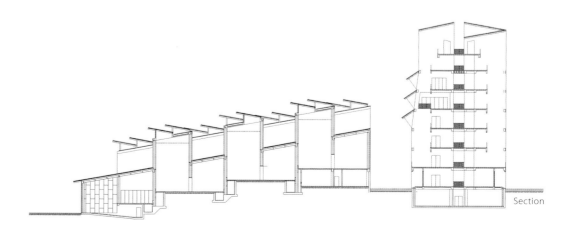

Section

4. Space between Academic
   Building and Gallery
5. Academic Building façade detail
6. First floor passage in Hall
   of Graduate Studies

6

7

7. Entrance hall in the Gallery
8. Gallery interior

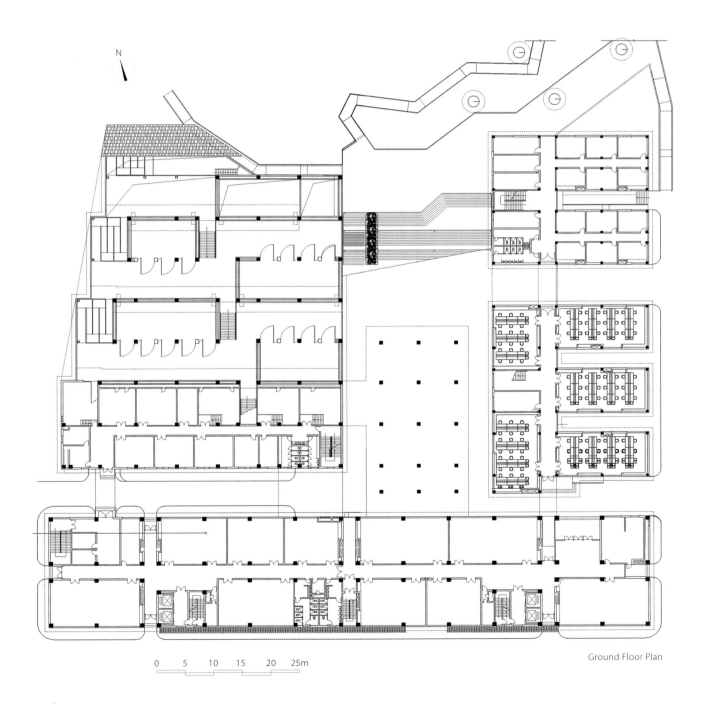

N

0   5   10   15   20   25m

Ground Floor Plan

BUPT STUDENT DORMITORY AND CANTEEN
Beijing
SDG (Shine Design Group Pty. Ltd.)

Site Area: 36,800m²
Gross Floor Area: 55,300m²
Design/Completion Time: 2005/2006
Architect: SDG (Shine Design Group Pty. Ltd.)
Design Team: NIE Jianxin, CHEN Xiangqing
Photographer: SDG (Shine Design Group Pty. Ltd.)
Client: BUPT

Master Plan

The Beijing University of Posts and Telecommunications (BUPT) is located in Haidian Disctrict, Beijing. The student dormitory is built at the north part of the campus, with a sports field on the east, Hongfu Middle School on the west, BUPT teaching section on the south, and Hongfu Community on the north.

The dormitory complex is composed of a series of buildings organised around the central "water belt" as an axis. On both sides of the axis three semi-closed dormitory buildings are located. The west ones are oriented on a north-south direction, in accordance to the adjacent existing buildings on the west, while the east ones are placed parallel to the main teaching building. Each semi-closed building defines a space for students, contributing to privacy and independency. Each space has its own qualities which give the users a sense of belonging.

On the east side of the central axis are five-storey buildings, lower than the west side ones (six storeys). The one at the northeast corner is the highest building with nine storeys, acting as the focal point of the complex.

Architectural Design

Due to the long history of the site, the architects decided to adopt grey bricks on the façade to create a special air that belongs to traditional Chinese architecture. The random pattern on the brick façade is intended to resemble information code, since these buildings serve for the College of Software. As for the nine-storey building at the northeast corner, pre-fabricated cladding panels are used, resulting in a low cost and short construction period. Furthermore, the colour of the panels is similar to that of the grey bricks, so it looks as if they are grey bricks with a big scale, creating a unified, harmonious context.

The grey bricks are slightly different in colour and shape, and are selected according to the users. The three buildings on the west are dormitories for men, the two on the east are for women, and the nine-storey one is a high-standard dormitory. Correspondingly, dark grey bricks are mainly used on men's dormitories, with randomly inserted light grey bricks; light grey ones are used on women's dormitories, with randomly inserted dark

Rendering

1. Dormitory façade facing the river
2. Overview of dormitory buildings
3. Façade of female student dormitory

Dormitory #1 and #2 West Elevation

Dormitory #1 and #2 East Section

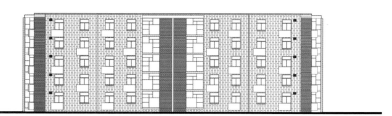

Dormitory #1 and #2 East Elevation

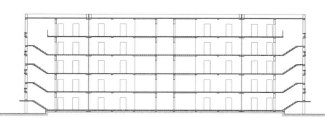

Dormitory #1 and #2 West Section

grey ones; as for the high-standard dormitory, Qomolangma pre-fabricated panels are used with a balanced combination of dark and light grey. The architects didn't want to make the buildings look too rational or mechanical, and therefore they adopted yellow panels for the balconies on the west three buildings to bring out a lively air, since the users are vigorous young students. The east two buildings have "peeling surfaces" on particular positions, making them appear more beautiful since they are women dormitories. The high-standard dormitory has yellow panels on its façade for ornamentation.

BUPT Student Canteen

The canteen has a total floor area of 2,300 square metres, with three storeys above ground. It is a steel structure clad in large-scale pre-fabricated panels, with a grey tone to correspond with the adjacent dormitory complex. The wavy folding boards on the façade are a metaphorical architectural language reflecting both the waterscape of the site and the vivacious characteristics of students. The monolithic structure resembling a bookshelf gets an industrial feel from inside through to outside, and it is easy for both construction and utilisation.

Dormitory #5 Sections

Dormitory #5 Ground Floor Plan:
1. Dorm
2. Balcony
3. Corridor
4. Activity room
5. Lift
6. Barrier-free ramp
7. Cleaning room
8. Fire fighting control
9. Service room
10. Duty room

4. Foreign student dormitory building façade
5. Northeast view of foreign student dormitory building
6. Foreign student dormitory building façade detail

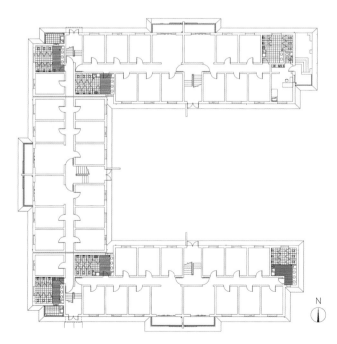

Dormitory #1 and #2 Floor Plan

7. Canteen overview
8. Canteen façade
9. Canteen interior

Canteen Elevation (A)
(Slot: 5mm Wide,
with the Same Colour as
Corresponding Façade):
1. Grey metal paint (matt)
2. Greyish white metal paint (glossy)
3. Grey metal paint (matt)
4. Greyish white metal paint (glossy)
5. Folding panel
6. Black aluminium frame
7. Black aluminium swing door

Canteen Section (B):
1. Double glazing, white
2. Smoke outlet, with
   white louvre inside
3. White
4. Glass panel
5. Grey aluminium edge

Canteen Elevation (C):
(Slot: 5mm Wide,
with the Same Colour as
Corresponding Façade):
1. Yellow metal paint
2. Grey metal paint
3. Blue metal paint
4. Aluminium louvre, on the
   same surface with façade
   Surface paint with the same
   colour as corresponding façade

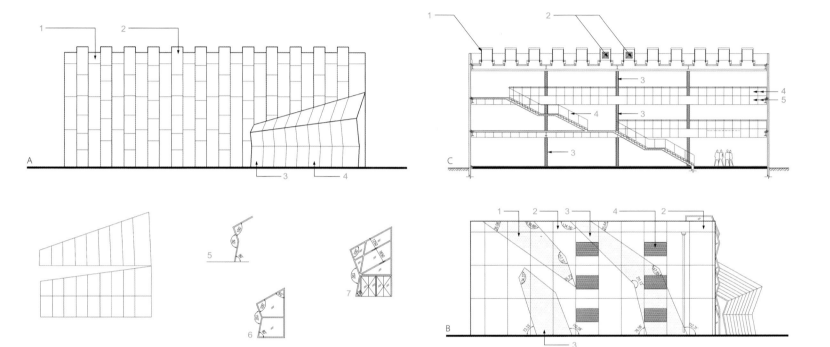

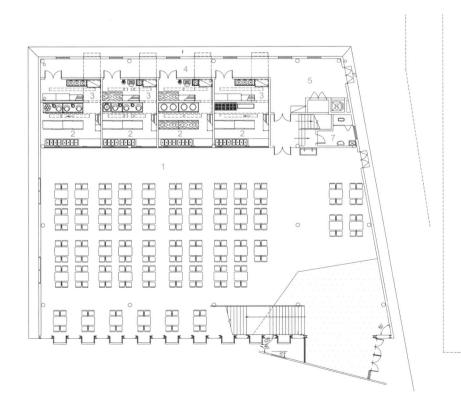

Canteen First Floor Plan:
1. Dining hall
2. Preparation room
3. Preliminary preparation
4. Corridor
5. Wardrobe
6. Lift for food
7. Toilet

043

FINE ARTS SCHOOL
IN CHINA CENTRAL ACADEMY OF FINE ARTS
Beijing
SYN Architects

Gross Floor Area: 136,000m²
Design/Completion Time: 2005/2007
Architect: SYN Architects
Photographer: SYN Architects
Client: China Central Arts University

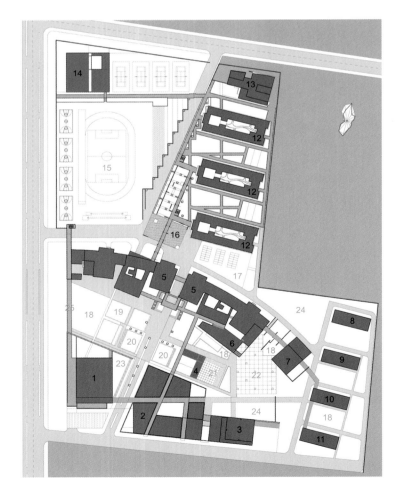

The new 136,000-square-metre campus of the Fine Arts School in China Central Academy of Fine Arts is located to the north-east of Beijing. The existing campus in Beijing couldn't meet the need of development of the Academy, and thus a new campus was initiated, which would accommodate some schools in the Academy such as the Postgraduate School and an attached middle school.

Some buildings of the ensemble had been structurally completed when SYN Architects was getting involved in the project. The current completed new buildings consist of extensions to the main building, a refectory, connecting bridges and the entrance building. In addition, the landscape and the sporting fields had been designed and made. Connected with bridges, courtyards are placed among the volumes to bring daylight and fresh air into the building. Big gaps between the studios and the practice rooms and a varying façade design generate the impression of being in an ensemble rather than standing in front of a space-consuming wall.

Site Plan (Left):
1. Library
2. Gallery
3. Complex Building
4. Office Building
5. Teaching Building
6. Terrace
7. Clubhouse
8. Staff Apartment #1
9. Staff Apartment #2
10. Staff Apartment #3
11. Staff Apartment #4
12. Female students dorm
13. Refectory
14. Sports facility
15. Sports field
16. Central plaza
17. Car park
18. Lawn
19. Landscape plaza
20. Waterscape
21. Sunken plaza
22. Sculpture garden
23. Sunken courtyard
24. Greenery
25. Bridges

For campus landscape, the architects were inspired by traditional Chinese gardens. A lot of leisure spaces are created among buildings and bridges. Artists as well as students can enjoy the beautiful scenery there, and will be surprised with new discoveries from time to time. Ever-changing views are attached with great importance in design. Living in the campus would be a pleasure, and your perception towards it would be always enriched.

The centre of the existing shell construction was pulled down to create a representative entrance. Three partly glazed bridges generate an attractive situation and will connect the administration building (second construction phase) with the dormitories and the sporting grounds. In the second construction phase there will be a tribune and sport field, as well as an arena, gallery, administration building, houses for teachers and a hotel.

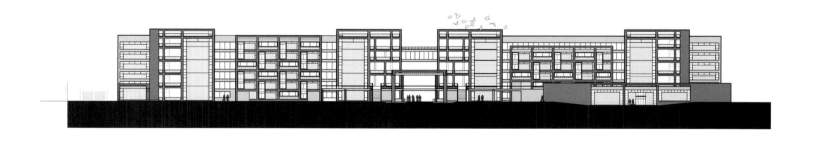

Main Building Elevations

1. Different façade structures
   make the buildings readable
2. Perspective of front elevation
3. Main entrance detail
4. View through the main entrance
   to the housing units

Main Building Sections

3

4

5, 6. Student housing units
7. The Academy after
   the first design stage

Area of Main Buildings

Movement Bridges

Movement – Free Space

New Buildings – New Plazas

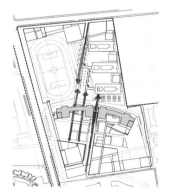

New Opening

Outer Movement

Inner Movement

Study – Live

8. Bridges connecting the student
   housing units with the whole campus
9. Bridges connecting the different
   areas of the campus
10. Gallery
11. Bridges protecting from sun and rain
12. Courtyard of the student housing units

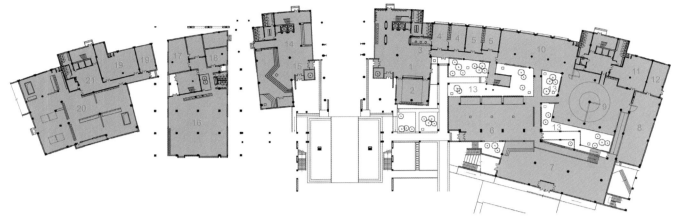

Ground Floor Plan:
1. East vestibule
2. Reception office
3. Reception
4. Dean's office
5. Gallery office
6. Exhibition Hall A
7. Exhibition Hall B
8. Exhibition Hall C
9. Exhibition Hall D
10. Exhibition Hall E
11. Temporary storeroom
12. Exhibition hall storeroom
13. Courtyard
14. West vestibule
15. Shop (art materials and books)
16. Engraving studio
17. Engraving teaching and research office
18. Service Centre
19. Sculpture teaching and research office
20. Sculpture studio
21. Washing room

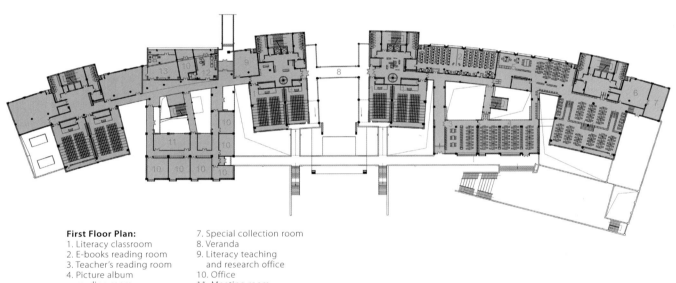

First Floor Plan:
1. Literacy classroom
2. E-books reading room
3. Teacher's reading room
4. Picture album reading room
5. Office and catalogue room
6. Reading room
7. Special collection room
8. Veranda
9. Literacy teaching and research office
10. Office
11. Meeting room
12. President office
13. Guest reception room

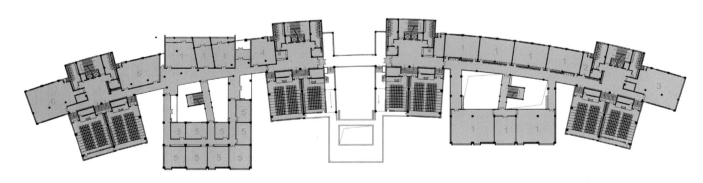

Second Floor Plan:
1. Painting room
2. Pre-function room
3. Skill classroom
4. Teaching tools storeroom
5. Office
6. Students' works collection room

12

ART GALLERY IN SHENZHEN UNIVERSITY
Shenzhen, Guangzhou Province
QIN Li / QL Studio

Gross Floor Area: 2,400m²
Design/Completion Time: 2007/2008
Architect: QIN Li / QL Studio
Design Team: LUO Jingjing, WEN Yaqiao
Photographer: QIN Li
Client: Shenzhen University

The Art Gallery is located in Shenzhen University campus, with its north side facing the thoroughfare at the north entrance of the university. The gallery serves for students and professors in the Department of Art. The site was originally occupied by the iconic "Houses of Ghost" designed by Li Ruisheng, professor of the Department of Art.

Professor Li is not an architect himself, and the "Houses of Ghost" he designed were a complex with an inner courtyard in which lychee and bamboo are planted. The site, with a significant height difference (the west side higher than the east), enjoys a very beautiful environment. The houses were built with rubble stone, creating a unique silhouette. They used to be a well-known artistic studio in the campus, even in the city of Shenzhen. Due to some reason related to property right, the main building was demolished and temporary music classrooms and exhibition hall were built. The stone houses at the back of the courtyard were retained, and the new Art Gallery was built on the plot of the original main building facing the north entrance. The site along the main ring road in the campus plays a significant role of landscaping for the university.

Due to the specific site condition, particularly the height difference, the architects chose flexible building forms to cope with the site. The architecture composed of small-scale modules is identical to the original "Houses of Ghost". A series of cubic modules, with different sizes and directions, constitute an irregular, complex composition. In this way, the whole architecture is integrated into the context, offering a strong sense of modernity. The irregular layout and flexible composition contribute to unconventional interior spaces, enlarge the exposed surfaces, and attract more attention with the unique silhouette. Therefore, the Art Gallery, though small in size, is given a unique identity, which makes it an eye-catching spot at the north entrance of the university.

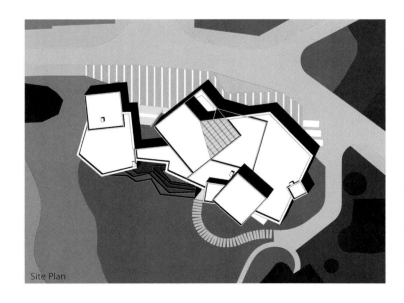
Site Plan

2

The architects took advantage of the height difference of the site, and made a three-dimensional integration of the architectural spaces and the surroundings. Big steps are designed in front of the main entrance, which leads to the atrium on the first floor of the Art Gallery. The main exhibition hall on the ground floor is connected to the inner courtyard by the outdoor sunken area (also used for exhibition). The exhibition halls are positioned in a linear way, simple and clear. The lobby and the lounge, with windows opening to the lychee forest, enjoy splendid views, while the interiors are closed space for the privacy of exhibitions. The exhibition spaces are organised in a dynamic, three-dimensional way, inter-connected to form a ring. In addition, several aerial corridors and two-storey spaces are created to enrich the interior because the architects believe that exhibition architecture should have various forms of spaces.

The newly built Art Gallery is part of the so-called "Art Village" in which several rubble stone houses are retained. Therefore, the architects have to establish a proper relationship between the Art Gallery and the old buildings, in terms of building form and scale. Besides, the innovative elements in the old buildings, such as material and construction technique, should be kept in new architecture. Hence, with a budget of only 3,000,000 RMB, the architects decided to use cheap natural materials such as rubble stone and timber. In this way, the new building and the old ones are consistent in material. Meanwhile, artificial material – expansive frameless glass – is adopted to combine with the natural materials, making the spaces feel more open and modern.

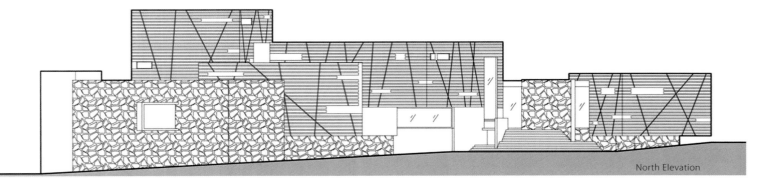

North Elevation

1. Northeast façade
2. Bird's-eye view
3. Perspective
4. Main entrance
5. Southwest view
6. Southeast view
7. Courtyard

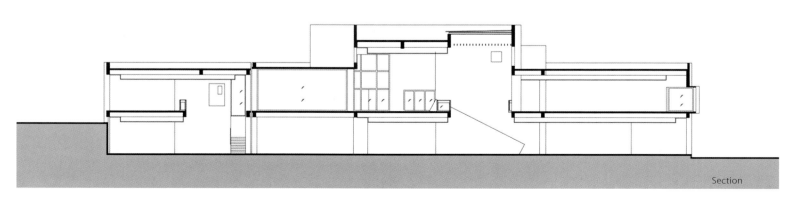

Section

7

8. Courtyard landscape
9. Natural lighting in the exhibition hall

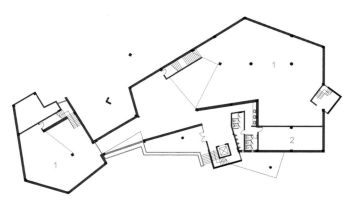

Ground Floor Plan:
1. Exhibition hall
2. Electric room

First Floor Plan:
1. Exhibition hall
2. Void
3. Lounge
4. Conversation room

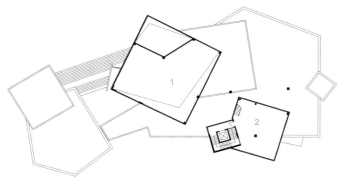

Second Floor Plan:
1. Void
2. Storage

LEO KOGUAN BUILDING, FACULTY OF LAW, PEKING UNIVERSITY
Beijing
Andrea Destefanis, Filippo Gabbiani / Kokaistudios

Gross Floor Area: 10,000m²
Completion Time: 2010
Architect: Andrea Destefanis, Filippo Gabbiani / Kokaistudios
Project Responsible: LI Wei
Design Team: FANG Weiyi, LIU Wenwen, YU Feng
Structural Engineer/Mechanics & Electricity: BIAD
Photographer: Charlie Xia
Client: The Leo KoGuan Foundation, the United States of America

Balance Architecture with Light

A challenging project for the most prestigious university in China in the heart of its historical campus.

In 2009, a prestigious American Foundation (The Leo KoGuan Foundation) and Peking University invited Kokaistudios to design the building for the new faculty of law located in a prestigious location within the historical campus of China leading university. This particular site, where the pagoda symbol of the university is standing, required considerable effort in terms of design in order to find architectural answers that could satisfy and meld in a harmonious way the heritage elements, the beautiful natural environment and the new contemporary building. This prestigious project is considered the milestone of a new era for Peking University, and a symbol for better and more environmentally sustainable standard of living for the future university community and for architectural buildings within that community.

This project has been conceived on a rigid volumetric shape imposed by the strict regulation protecting the historical site and at the same time by the necessity to fulfill all the functional requirements of the new faculty. The rigorous style requested to be accepted by the large number of heritage commissions have been interpreted in a creative way by Kokaistudios by proposing an elegant use of few materials, concrete plasters and local stones with capabilities to transmit daylight and a clever use of skylights and sinking gardens in order to increase the use of natural light and thermal efficiency of the building. Kokaistudios transformed the façades to become light filters and diffusing soft daylight all over the interiors. The entire system of internal spaces has been designed by the team so as to upgrade the standards of working, living, and studying of the future professors and students, using sustainable materials and creating aggregation facilities and spaces that could satisfy the flexible demands of the faculty in the future.

Site Plan:
1. Entrance
2. Access to garage
3. Micro-electronics Building
4. Building #1, Faculty of Law
5. Guanghua School of
   Management, phase II
6. Green plaza

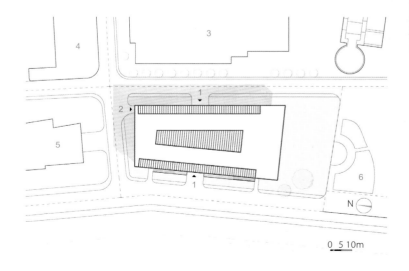

0 5 10m

1. Façade night view
2. Building daytime view
3. Building night view
4. Main façade detail

North Elevation

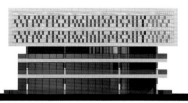

South Elevation

East Elevation

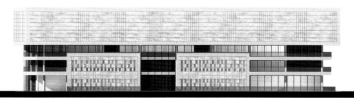

West Elevation

3

4

5

5. Sunken garden
6. Double-height hallway

Sections (Right and Facing Below):
1. Lobby
2. Passage/extension of Simulated Court
3. Rest
4. Info
5. Simulated Court
6. Office
7. Study room
8. Reading room
9. M&E room

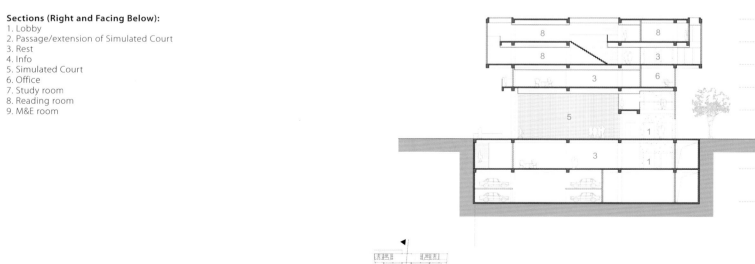

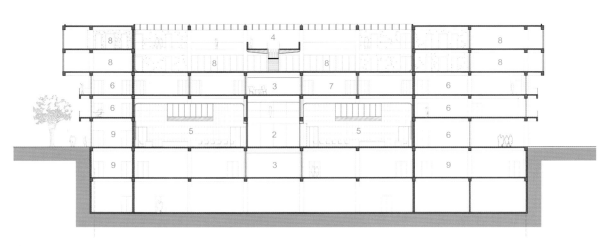

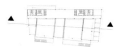

7. Entrance lobby
8. Court hall

Ground Floor Plan:
1. Main entrance
2. Lobby
3. Passage/extension of Simulated Court
4. Simulated Court
5. Office
6. Meeting room
7. Toilet
8. M&E room
9. Fire control centre

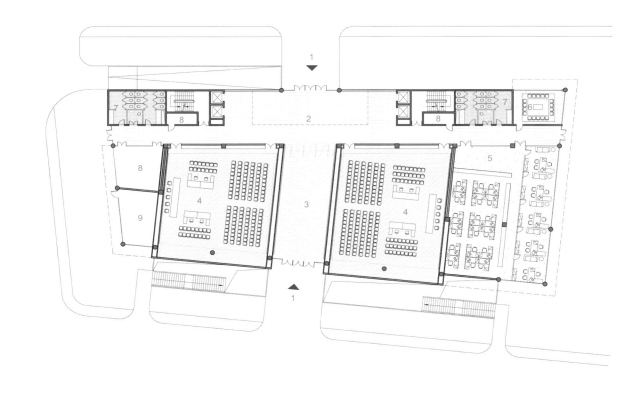

Third Floor Plan:
1. Rest
2. Office
3. Meeting room
4. Study room
5. Toilet
6. M&E room

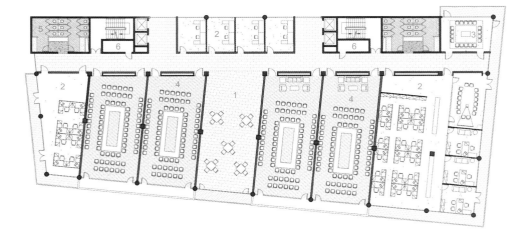

9

9, 10. Library

Fourth Floor Plan:
1. Rest
2. Info
3. Office
4. Reading room
5. Toilet
6. M&E room

Fifth Floor Plan:
1. Rest
2. Info
3. Reading room
4. Toilet
5. M&E room

TEACHING COMPLEX AT HUNAN UNIVERSITY
Changsha City, Hunan Province
Hunan University Design Institute, Co., Ltd.

Site Area: 12,582m²
Gross Floor Area: 20,997m²
Design/Completion Time: 2007/2009
Architect: Hunan University Design Institute, Co., Ltd.
Design Team: WEI Chunyu, LI Xu, YANG Yuehua
Photographer: QIANG Wei, XU Haohao
Client: Hunan University

Background

Hunan University has a long history. The existing campus occupies an area of 1,462,000m², with a gross floor area of 819,000m², providing teaching, research and living facilities for the University. In recent years the University has been developing with a fast pace, and a new campus was in need to meet requirements of teaching and research. Therefore, a site of 138,000m² south of the existing campus was chosen to hold the new campus, where the Teaching Complex was the first architecture to be built, setting a context for future construction of the campus. Design of the project started from May 2007, and construction was completed on August 2008.

Master Plan

The existing campus was planned with two axes perpendicular to each other: the one that starts from Yuelu Academy and ends at the entrance near Xiang River is called "art axis", and the other is called "science axis", from which the new campus plan took reference. In the new campus, the axis starts from Faculty of Law, goes through School of Civil Engineering, Engineering Laboratory, College of Software, Science and Technology Building, and ends at Teaching Complex. The axis makes a turn at the playing field, organising the spaces in sequence. The Teaching Complex was sited at the south part of the new campus, with Fubuhe Road to the west (with disorderly commercial facilities on the other side of the road), Science and Technology Building to the south (in plan), Tianma Mountain to the east, and Student Apartments to the south. The Teaching Complex acts as the final end of the axis.

Layout and Circulation

The Teaching Complex, as the name suggests, provides teaching facilities for the University, including classrooms at different sizes (for 60, 100, 150 and 300 people), individual study rooms, and offices, bicycle parking on air, totaling approx. 20,000m² in floor area. The general layout is I-shaped, with the vertical line spanning 116.64m and the horizontal 53.88m. Horizontal circulation is completed with corridors and bridges, being, continuous and active. Eight staircases are well distributed, providing efficient vertical circulation.

The site has a small height difference: the northwest part of the site is 2.25m lower than the Fubuhe Road, and the southwest part is on the same level with the road. The complex separates pedestrians and vehicles according to the existing condition of the site. The plaza on the west is connected with the Fubuhe Road, and pedestrians are guided to the ground floor hallway by steps. Vehicles enter the campus from the road on the southwest, and are parked by the road. Nearby is a bicycle parking lot on air, with entry and exit conveniently placed near the campus entrance. In this way, interference between pedestrians and vehicles is minimised.

Site Plan

Design with Logic
Logic in Design Theory: Group Composition

Group Composition explores how to integrate individual buildings into a group as a whole. In an era when university buildings need flexibility to meet new requirements, such a theory naturally came out. It is applied to the new campus plan to achieve a high efficiency in resource consumption. Group composition goes well with contemporary education concepts, which require easy interdisciplinary communication. Meanwhile, the integration of buildings must result in the re-integration of the building context, where landscapes overlap and various interesting places are created. The Teaching Complex is the starting point in the master plan of the new campus, and it doesn't have a complicated architectural form; instead, it acts as a compositional element in the group, though being identical, and prepares for the future "organic growing" of the group.

Logic in the Site: Turning Sideways

How to make the complex with a gross floor area of about 20,000m² integrate into the existing site is the primary issue the architects face; there are direct or indirect requirements from the site, which are quite difficult to coordinate. If you are confined within the site, probably your mind would be restricted; however, when you see the site as a part of the city, you would be enlightened at once. The Tianma Mountain on the east is the key in solving the primary issue. It should never be the landscape resource solely for the site, and therefore, the architects decided to let the complex turn sideways in order not to block sight of the beautiful mountain scenery. In this way, the mountain landscape

returns to serve the whole city. In addition, the linear composition of the complex acts as guidance to lead your sight towards the mountain. Therefore, the landscape is strengthened by the architecture, while the former acts as a background for the latter, giving prominence to its outline. The contradiction between the architecture and the mountain is solved and the two coexist in a harmonious way.

Logic in Composition: Linear Interspersion

Due to the requirements of group composition and different programmes, linear composition became the best solution. An aerial view shows clearly that the composition is quite easy: two square blocks perpendicular to urban roads compose the main part of the

2

1. North façade
2. Northeast perspective

complex; the block at the entrance is a horizontal one and projects out on the north, connecting the main bodies directly and forming a three-section compound (traditional Chinese residential composition); the two parts near the mountain are indirectly connected by a linking bridge, which is the best place to have a sweeping view of the mountain. The two extruded sides of the entrance seem to welcome visitors by a hug. The part in-between seems to recede with good arrangement, reducing psychosocial pressure towards the urban space. Seen from the urban road, the linear interspersion with twist and turn makes the complex vary in appearance. Flower terraces, steps, ramps, etc. follow the composition of the complex, and are interspersed in a pleasant way, echoing the wavy mountain in the distance. Meanwhile, the linear interspersion of the complex sets the base of the buildings and makes them "embedded" into the site. The comparatively complicated base forms some blurry places within the complex, which are not created on purpose and thus have no definite functions, but here are places where beautiful stories happen…

Logic in Space: Penetration

The architectural compound forms various enclosed spaces: the entrance plaza is open and active, with guiding steps; the inner courtyard is quiet and private, where, unconventionally, greenery is not the choice; instead, paving is done with the same material as the building façade to achieve a unified visual effect; seen from the courtyard, view of the mountain is framed by the building outlines, like the courtyard in Salk Institute by Louis Kahn. The big plaza at the entrance, the plaza before the complex and the plazas among the buildings are created at different levels and thus enrich the environment of the complex. Meanwhile, big steps, terraces and linking bridges are adopted to have a three-dimensional connection among buildings in the complex. In this way, spaces above and under ground, interior and exterior, building and scenery, people and architecture penetrate each other, forming a subtle relationship. Gardens on air are created by having "subtraction" on the façades, enriching the environment and creating a close relationship with the Tianma Mountain and the campus landscape. Penetration not only enriches spaces of the complex, but also improves its eco performance. The levels built on stilts and the open-air courtyards are combined to connect interior and exterior spaces together, achieving natural ventilation and a good cooling effect. In the meanwhile, inspired by traditional residences in the west of Hunan Province – the stilted house, the architects draw daylight and natural air in from side halls, improving micro-climate effectively. Compared with expensive eco-technology, these plain solutions are suitable for current circumstances in China, and reveal the architects attempts to explore local architecture in their design.

Logic in Material: Granitic Plaster

The architects are faced with two issues: one is how to embed local culture in the architecture, and the other is how to cope with the limited budget. Hunan University has a history of more than 1,000 years, so the architecture must show respect to local culture. Simple imitation of the old buildings in the existing campus or repetition of its iconic landmarks would be a superficial solution. Moreover, with a limited budget, distortion of building form or using new materials to present a modern building would be impossible. Finally, material became the breakthrough point. After making every effort in seeking and comparing materials, the architects chose granitic plaster for the façades, the material used in the old buildings in the existing campus. With natural light, granitic plaster has diffuse reflection and refraction effects, which present different colours and textures in seasons with different weathers and angles of light. Moreover, the granitic plaster surfaces make the buildings look worn out and thus integrate into the environment naturally. It helps define a field with a unified material and texture, a field where the architecture "grows out". With the rough surfaces, the buildings seem a bit primitive, and clear glass partially embedded into the buildings creates a dramatic effect. This unconventional approach makes the complex identical and distinguishes it from the disorderly surrounding buildings. The strip windows (W:L=1:4) are regularly and vertically arranged on the façades. The openings are caved in dramatically to create long shadows, and the "caves" make the complex look like a giant sculpture. There are parts inserted into or extruded from the façades, adding variation to the unified context. You can find traces of the old campus in the complex, while the contemporary composition reveals its status as a landmark in the region.

3

Conclusion

The logic in design makes the architecture somewhat self-disciplinary, revealing the architects' exploration in place, space, material, and the like. Logic guarantees architectural quality, and at times you would be unexpectedly touched. After completion, you can observe people enjoying leisure near the Teaching Complex. They stand, sit or recline near the flower terraces, on the steps, and in the roof garden. They can read, talk and look far into the distance with warm sunshine. These scenes go beyond the original conception of the architects, but they are quite glad to see.

3. Southwest perspective
4. Southeast perspective

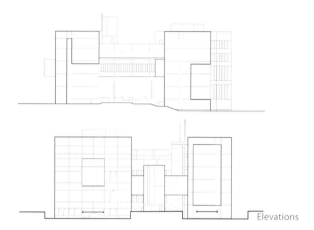

Elevations

4

5. Main entrance on the west
6. Courtyard on the east

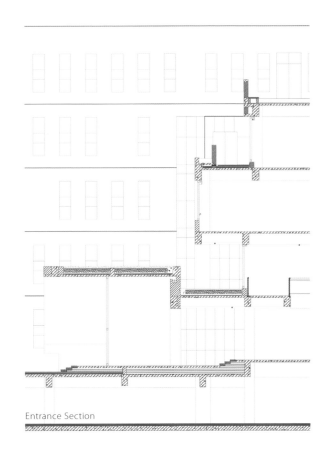

Entrance Section

7. Entrance ramp
8. Staircase in the garden on air

Ground Floor Plan:
1. Passageway
2. Teaching Building entrance
3. Lobby
4. Lecture hall (capacity: 240)
5. Classroom (capacity: 100)
6. Lift lobby
7. Male toilet
8. Female toilet
9. Teachers' lounge
10. Lecture hall (capacity: 300)
11. Lecture hall (capacity: 160)
12. Reception
13. Classroom (capacity: 80)

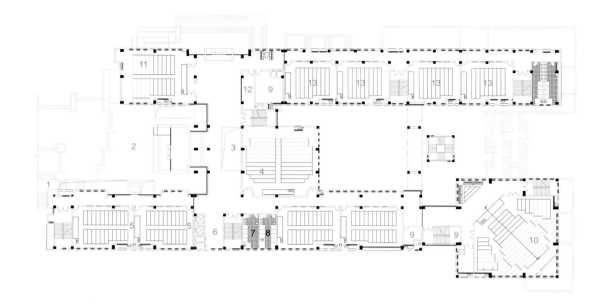

First Floor Plan:
1. Classroom (capacity: 100)
2. Teachers' lounge
3. Lecture hall (capacity: 300)
4. Lecture hall (capacity: 240)
5. Lecture hall (capacity: 160)
6. Office
7. Classroom (capacity: 80)
8. Individual study room

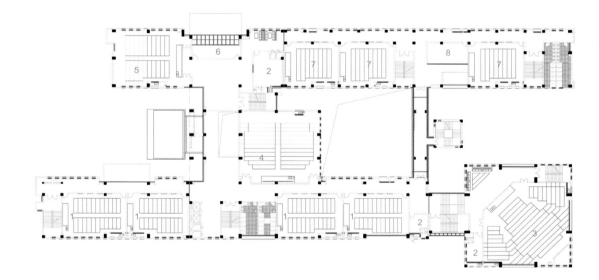

Second Floor Plan:
1. Classroom (capacity: 100)
2. Office
3. Lecture hall (capacity: 240)
4. Lecture hall (capacity: 160)
5. Classroom (capacity: 80)
6. Individual study room

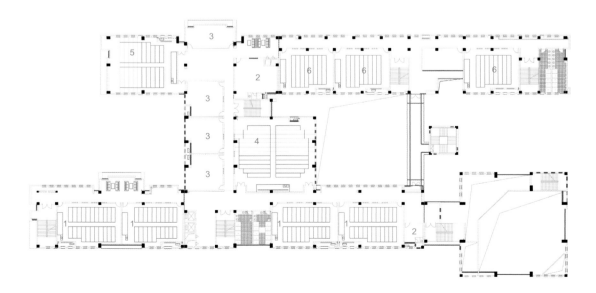

LIBRARY IN SICHUAN FINE ART INSTITUTE, HUXI CAMPUS
Chongqing
TANG Hua / Tang Hua Architectural Design Co., Ltd., Shenzhen

Gross Floor Area: 14,259.44m²
Design/Completion Time: 2006/2008
Architect: TANG Hua / Tang Hua Architectural Design Co., Ltd., Shenzhen
Technical Design: SU Weidong / Chongqing Architectural Design Institute
Structure: Reinforced Concrete Frame
Photographer: TANG Hua, XU Lang, Fu Xing Architectural Photography

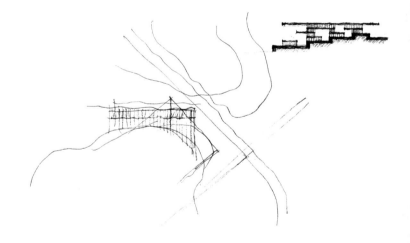

The Library in Sichuan Fine Art Institute, Huxi Campus is located at the central area between teaching sector and living sector. The site is an east-west stretching terrace, with a maximum height difference of six metres and hills no more than twenty metres high on the north and south side. The east of the site is connected to the thoroughfare in the campus. The brief of the Library is to have the capacity of 1,200 seats and one million books.

The Library is positioned with a north-south direction, vertical to the contour of the terrace. The slice volume contributes to good performance in natural lighting and ventilation, and also provides a continuous view of landscape for the interior.

Sichuan Fine Art Institute is firmly based on the local culture, which greatly influenced artists of different generations here who have been keen on exploring local traditions. The design of the Library is no exception. The configuration of the architecture is inspired by commonly seen buildings in Chongqing in the east of Sichuan Province, such as brickkilns and warehouses. The building stands out in the hilly area with a simple and integrated form, being in sharp contrast with the existing small and scattered buildings in the campus. The meaningful relationship between such an architectural form with a "local complex" and the intentionally preserved and designed agricultural landscape is obvious. The concise shape maximised the use of the interior space, which is similar to the layout of traditional architecture.

Materials are selected according to the building structure and, more importantly, to local history. The façades of the main building are constructed with blue clay bricks, which continue from the roof to the ground of the plaza. The interior walls, beams and columns are pure concrete without any decoration, being harmonious with the façades in terms of colour and texture, yet not monotonous. Timber is utilised both in the façades and interior staircases. For the gable walls and the "sky garden", glass is extensively used, making interior activities in the Library clearly visible from outside. The façade materials are dense, solid and imposing, while the interior is soft, fine and friendly.

1. A strip volume
2. The surroundings
3. North façade

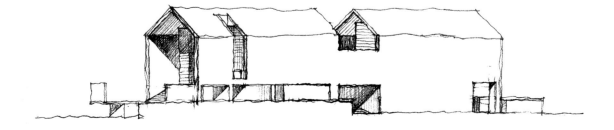

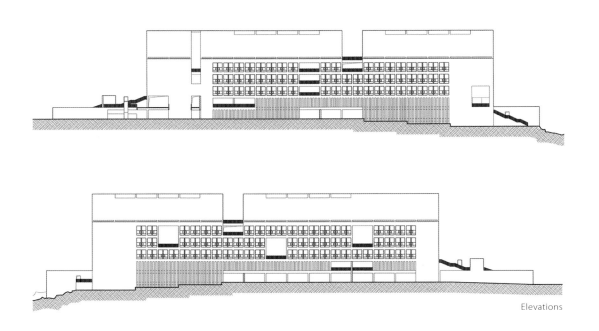

Elevations

4. West façade
5. Main path

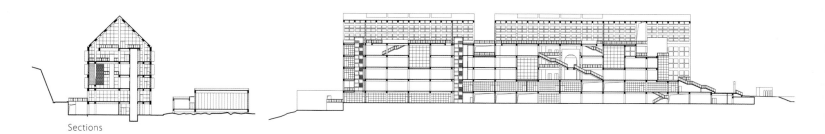

Sections

6-8. Main façades with cyan clay bricks

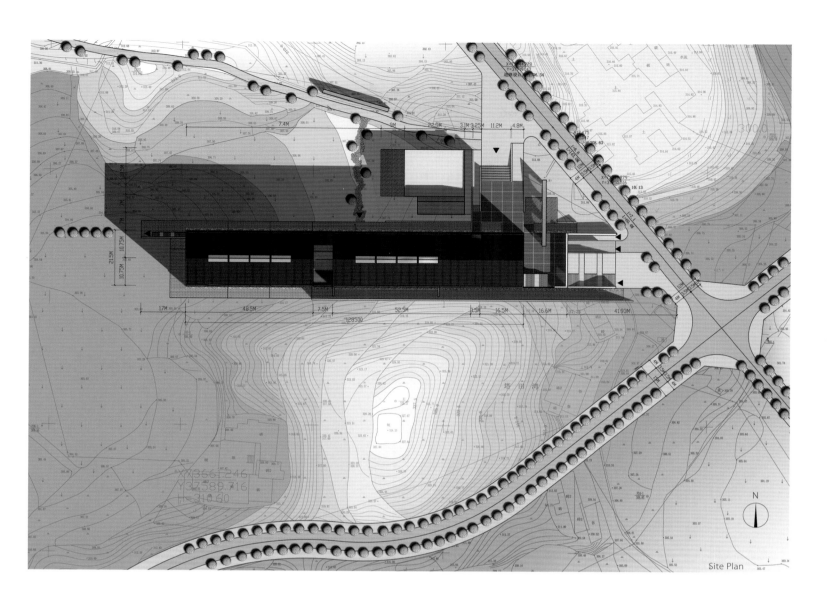

Site Plan

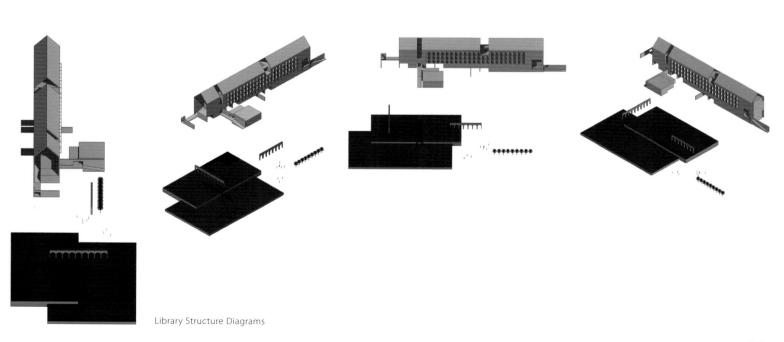

Library Structure Diagrams

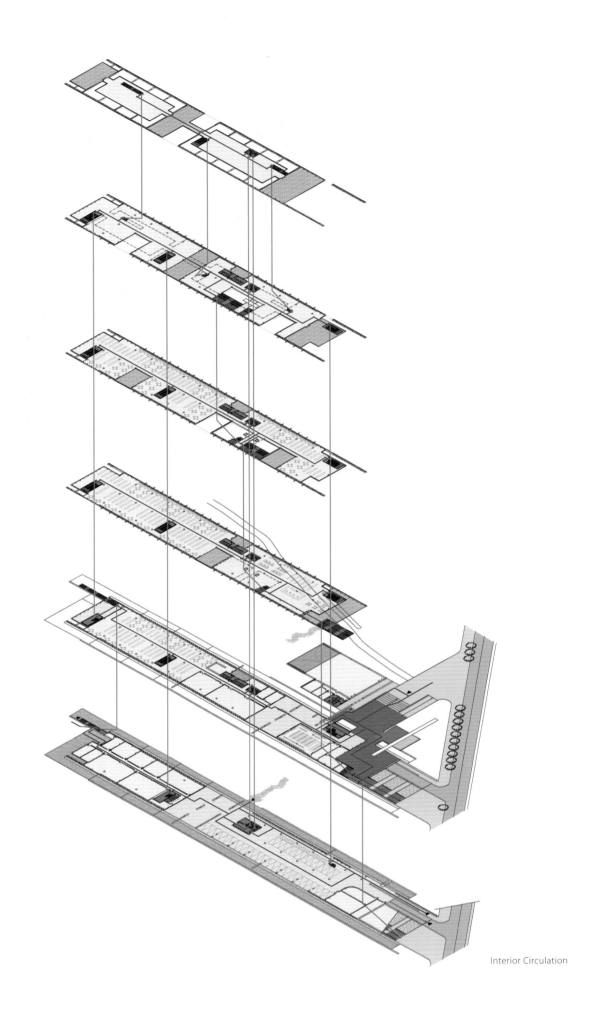

Interior Circulation

Basement Floor Plan:
1. Staff entrance
2. Underground garage entrance
3. Main entrance
4. Fire pool
5. Electrical facilities
6. Air conditioner
7. Underground garage
8. Dock
9. Lift lobby
10. Equipment room
11. Office facilities storage
12. Staff activity room
13. Training centre
14. Meeting room
15. Document centre
16. Deputy librarian office
17. Digital resource office
18. Information technology department
19. General affairs office
20. Librarian office
21. Outdoor terrace

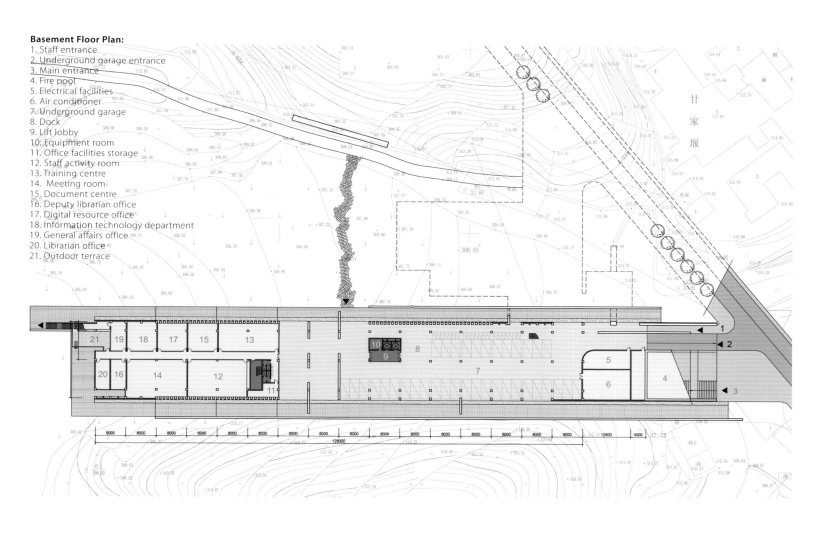

Ground Floor Plan:
1. Conference entrance
2. Temporary administration office vestibule
3. Academic lecture hall
4. Rest and preparation room
5. Security room
6. Main entrance
7. Underground garage entrance/exit
8. Staff entrance
9. Multi-functional hall
10. Outdoor terrace
11. VIP lounge
12. Equipment room
13. Storage
14. Library newsroom
15. Fine arts literature research department
16. Circulation and reading department
17. Restoration department
18. Editorial department
19. Back issues collection

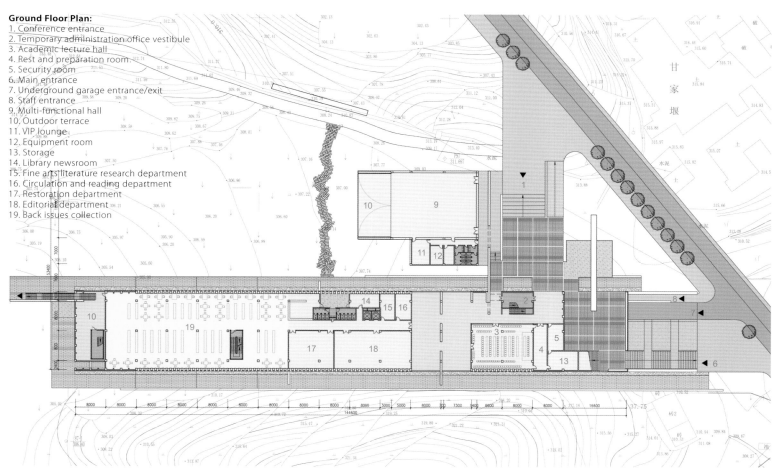

9. Building entrance
10. Stairs leading to top floor
11. The landscape of atrium
12. Interior walls, beams and
    columns with exposed concrete

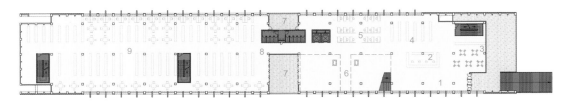

First Floor Plan (Above):
1. Lobby
2. Information desk
3. Water Bar
4. Bookshop
5. E-book reading room
6. Exhibition room
7. Garden
8. Non-book reading room
9. Current issues reading room

Second Floor Plan (Below):
1. Non-artistic books collection
2. Garden

13. Top floor skylight for natural lighting
14. Reading room on the top floor

**Third Floor Plan (Above) and
Mezzanine Floor Plan (Below):**
1. Temporary office
2. Garden

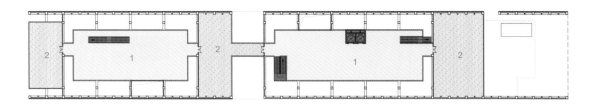

SINO-FRENCH CENTRE AT TONGJI UNIVERSITY
Shanghai
ZHOU Wei, ZHANG Bin / Atelier Z+

Site Area: 9,204m²
Building Area: 3,142m²
Gross Floor Area: 13,575m²
Design/Completion Time: 2004-2006/2006
Architect: ZHOU Wei, ZHANG Bin / Atelier Z+
Design Team: ZHUANG Sheng, LU Jun, WANG Jiaqi, XIE Jing
Contractor: Hua Sheng Construction (Group) Co., Ltd., Zhejiang
Photographer: ZHANG Siye
Client: Tongji University
Structure: Reinforced Concrete Frame, Partly Steel Frame;
Storeys: 1 Basement, 5 Storeys above Ground and 1-Storey Penthouse
Main Materials: COR-TEN Steel Sheet Panel, Precoated Cement Panel, Exposed Concrete, Steel Profile, Aluminium, Glass, Timber

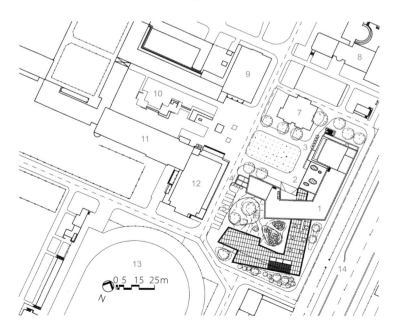

Sino-French Centre at Tongji University is located at the southeast corner of the campus, with The December 9th Movement Building, the oldest existing building of the campus, and The December 9th Movement Memorial Park on its west side, tracking field on its south side, and Siping Road on its east side. XuRi Building, which should be preserved, is located at the northwest corner of the site. Another precondition is that an existing forest of metasequoia and another nine trees scattered such as deodar cedars, planetrees, Japanese pagodatrees and willows should be retained.

Site Plan (Left):
1. Sino-French Centre, Tongji University
2. Main entrance
3. Secondary entrance
4. Garage entrance
5. Parking
6. Garden
7. Pavilion Xuri
8. Building of Science
9. Badminton court
10. The December 9th Movement Memorial Park
11. The December 9th Movement Memorial classroom
12. The December 9th Movement Memorial Salle
13. Sports field
14. Siping Road

2

The goal of the project is to create a form system to integrate its programme, its site context and its culture context. The architects' way to achieve it is to use a geometric diagram to control the materialisation of its programme and circulation, to conform to the site restriction, and also to indicate its symbolic meaning, the culture exchange between the two countries. The diagram of "Hand in Hand" is introduced to organise the whole building with its inherent structure of dualistic juxtaposition.

1. Crossing bridge
2. Overview from southwest
3. Southwest view

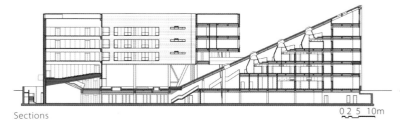

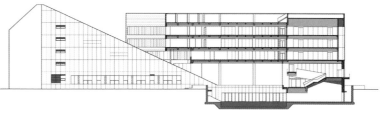

Sections   0 2 5 10m

The programme is composed of three parts: college, office and public gathering space. Two similar yet different zigzag volumes, occupied by college and office sector respectively, overlap and interlace each other, and then they are linked together by the volume of public gathering space on underground and upper level. College and office sector share the main entrance which is located at the void of the intersection of these two volumes, while public gathering space has its own lobby, which faces to roof pool and sunken garden, to connect underground exhibition hall and lecture hall on the upper level. The function of the college and offices is well kept in mind by using regular shapes for almost each unit. Yet applying zigzag corridors to connect these units creates abundant interests throughout inside and outside spaces. In the meanwhile, existing trees are incorporated into the design to add more charms to this complex.

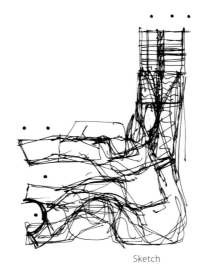

Sketch

4. View from west
5. View from north

Idea: Hand in Hand – A Structure of Dualistic Juxtaposition

Different materials and structures are applies to the different components of the complex. College sector is wrapped by COR-TEN steel sheet panels. The unique texture and colour of the panels and the smoothness of the glass create delicate variation. Pre-coated cement panel is introduced into the office sector. Regular and irregular window bands provide sunlight to the office unites and corridors. Public gathering space is created by the combination of both COR-TEN steel panel and pre-coated cement panel. The vivid colour and texture of COR-TEN steel panel is contracted with plain grey cement panel. This treatment indicates the symbolic meaning of this project, the juxtaposition of two different cultures.

Landscape design plays a very important role in this project. The retained existing metasequoias, surrounded by office sector, public gathering area and XuRi Building form an entry plaza of the complex. Connected with The December 9th Movement Memorial Park, this space will become a very important outdoor space to serve the entire campus. The connection between the two parts of the building formed a roof pool and a sunken garden, which becomes intermedium between urban space and campus space. A semi-private garden, created by college and office sector, gives a peaceful place for learninging and relaxing. Eventually, by applying different geometries, materials, colours and structures, the architects created a unique architectural piece that has the profound meaning of cultural exchange between China and France.

Ground Floor Plan (Below):
1. Pavilion XuRi
2. Entrance hall
3. Pool
4. Theatre with a seating capacity of 140
5. Amphitheatre with a seating capacity of 70
6. Classroom
7. Guard
8. Admissions office
9. Training Department
10. Male/female/handicapped toilet
11. Storage
12. Photocopy
13. Service
14. Electric room
15. Void

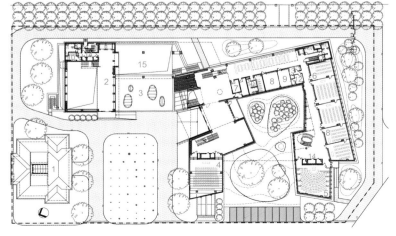

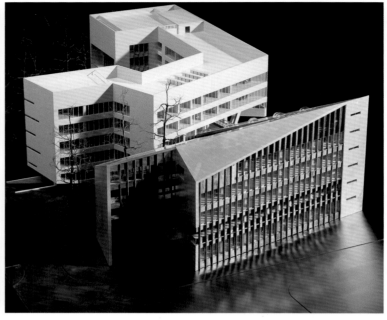

Models

7. Sunken garden

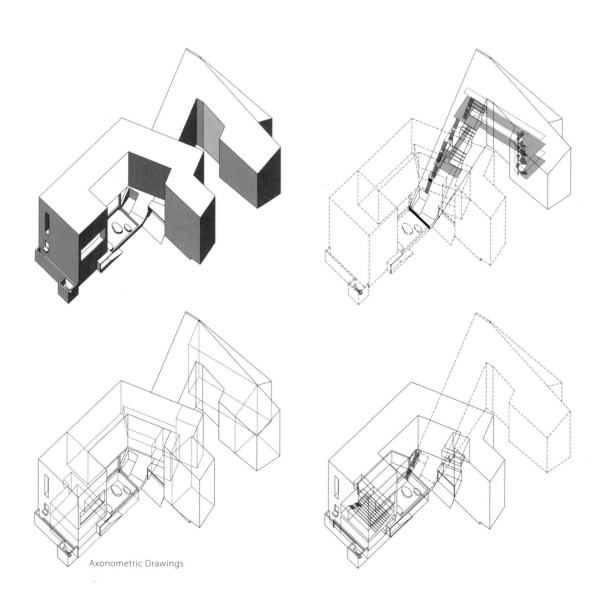

Axonometric Drawings

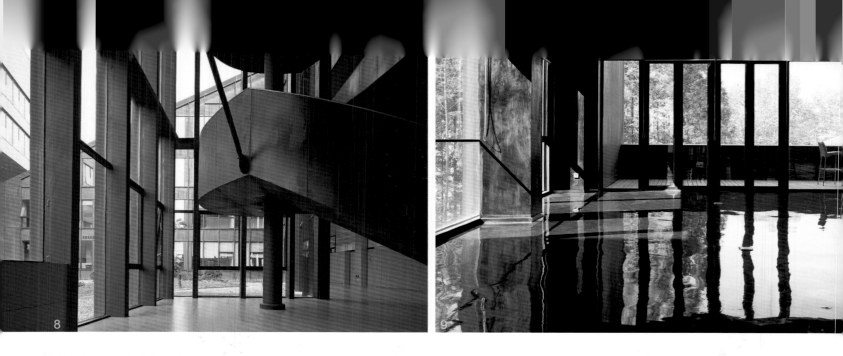

8. Spiral staircase in College Sector
9. Interior of public gathering space
10. Lecture hall
11. Terrace of College Sector
12, 13. Interior of Office Sector
14. Interior of College Sector

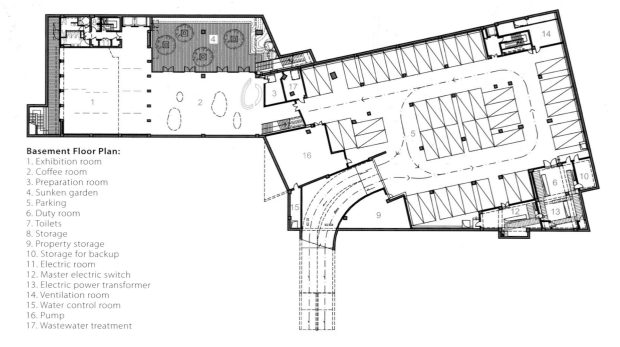

Basement Floor Plan:
1. Exhibition room
2. Coffee room
3. Preparation room
4. Sunken garden
5. Parking
6. Duty room
7. Toilets
8. Storage
9. Property storage
10. Storage for backup
11. Electric room
12. Master electric switch
13. Electric power transformer
14. Ventilation room
15. Water control room
16. Pump
17. Wastewater treatment

Second Floor Plan:
1. Multi-functional room
2. Office
3. Meeting room
4. Director's office
5. Amphitheatre
6. Pedagogy office
7. Teachers' lounge
8. Classroom
9. Consultant room
10. Secretary
11. Photocopy & fax
12. Service
13. Storage
14. toilets
15. Electric room
16. Crossing
17. Void

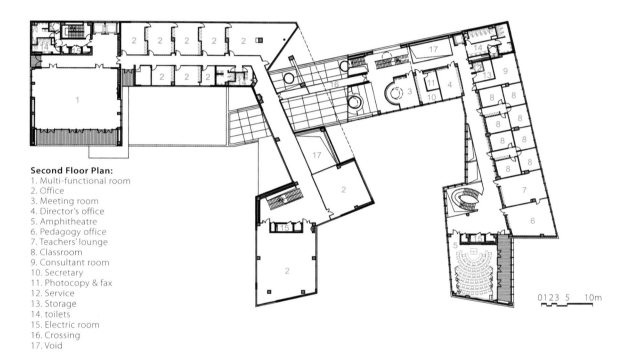

0 1 2 3 5   10m

GALLERY AT CHINA CENTRAL ACADEMY OF FINE ARTS
Beijing
Beijing New Era Architectural Design Ltd.

Site Area: 3,546m²
Gross Floor Area: 14,777m²
Design/Completion Time: 2004/2007
Architect: Beijing New Era Architectural Design Ltd.
Associate Architects: BArata Isozaki & Associates,
The Institute of Building Design of China Academy of Building Research
Photographer: Beijing New Era Architectural Design Ltd.
Client: China Central Academy of Fine Arts
Awards: Silver Award in the National Project Exploration and Design Award, 2010

The CAFA Gallery is located at the northeastern corner of the campus, in Wangjing district, Beijing. On a site occupying an area of 2,475 square metres, a six-storey frame-structure building (including two storeys underground), with a total floor area of 14,777 square metres, was built to accommodate various programmmes, including: plant room, storeroom, research room and fabrication room in the underground levels; lobby, lecture hall, café, meeting room and lounge on the ground floor; permanent exhibition hall on the first floor (divided into two parts: one housing ancient works of painting and calligraphy and paintings donated by retired senior professors from CAFA, and the other housing works of current professors); activity halls on the third and fourth floor.

The design of the gallery faced great challenge at the beginning. On one hand, galleries in Beijing generally have traditional architectural forms and exhibition spaces, unsuitable for large, contemporary works exhibition. Therefore, the client required a modern gallery for contemporary art exhibitions to meet international standards. On the other hand, in the new CAFA campus, buildings completed in phase 1 are all in a modest grey tone, with traditional architectural forms featuring rectangles and straight lines. Under such circumstances, this new gallery is required to present its identity and modernity, while at the same time being consistent with the existing buildings, balancing between unity and contrast.

The completed building is composed of three curving façades (with different curvature) and some rectangular bulges. The shape of the three-dimensional façades resembles a beautiful stroke in Chinese characters. The three vertical joining parts of the façades are the entry/exit of the exhibition hall, lecture hall, and back office respectively, while the horizontal joining part forms the roof. The delicate curving façades are perfectly integrated with the existing plot topography, elegant and dignified, and create interesting interiors for exhibition halls.

1. Façade material detail
2. Façade texture
3. Bird's-eye view

4. Projections mark building entrance

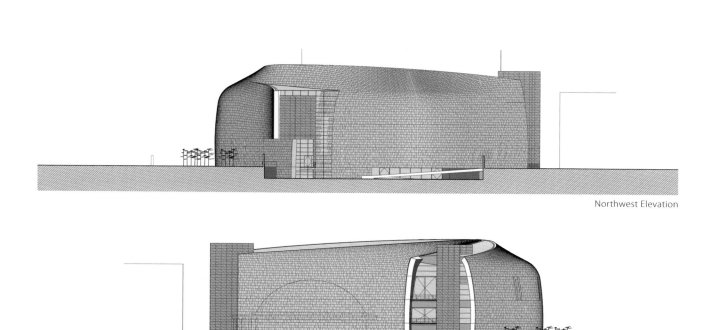

Northwest Elevation

Southeast Elevation

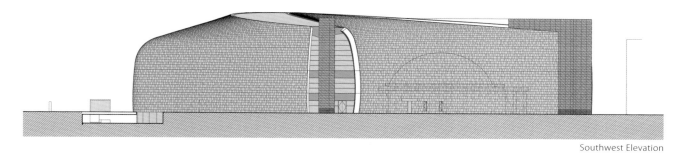

Southwest Elevation

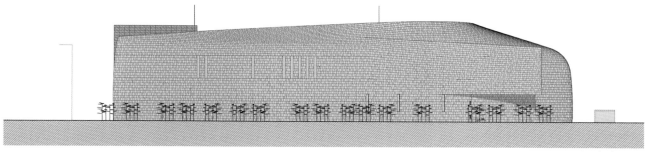

South Elevation

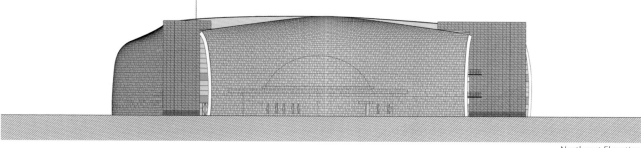

Northeast Elevation

5. Dome as a feature to blend roof and façade
6. Façade
7. Entrance detail
8. Entrance

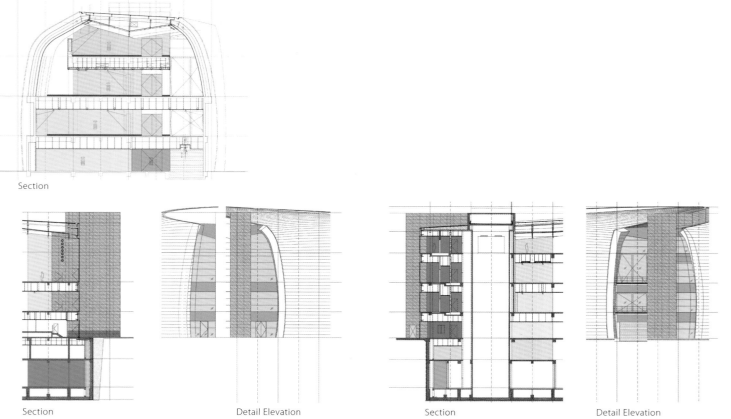

Section

Section

Detail Elevation

Section

Detail Elevation

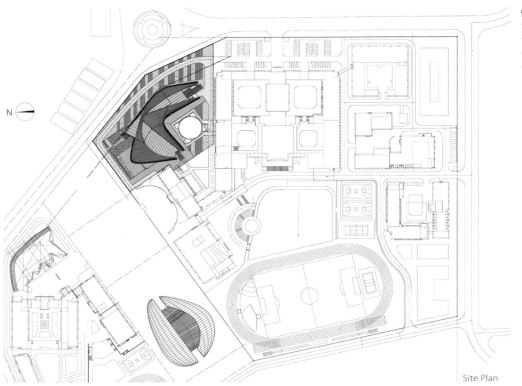

9. Contemporary Art Exhibition Hall on the second floor
10. Interior walls and skylight in the Exhibition Hall
11. Lobby
12. Skylight and ramp
13. Lounge outside the lecture hall

Site Plan

9

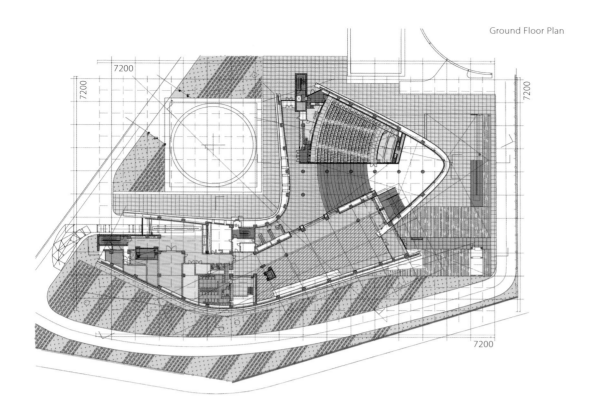

7200
7200
7200
7200

10

11

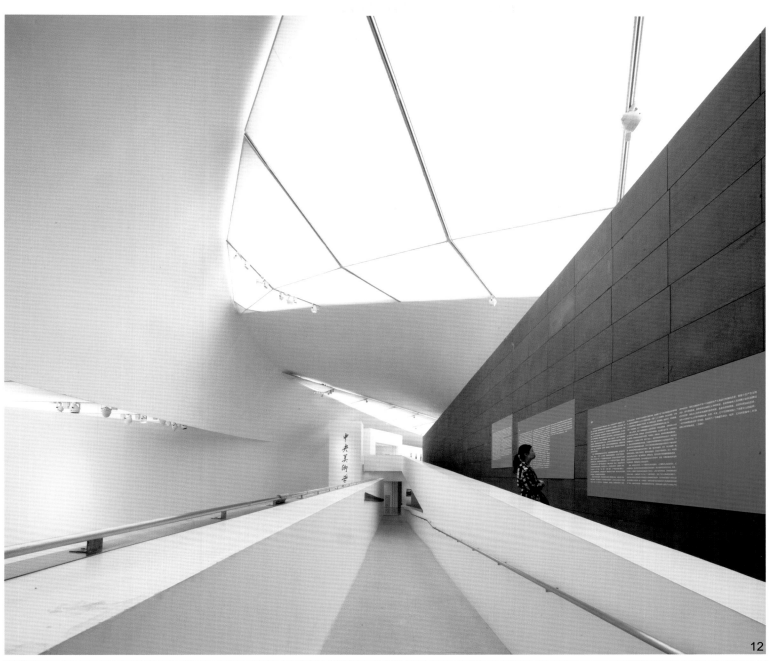

12

13

CICHENG HIGH SCHOOL
Jiangbei District, Ningbo, Zhejiang Province
DONG Yi / DC Alliance Pte Ltd, Singapore

Site Area: 68,900m²
Base Area: 11,368m²
Gross Floor Area: 11368m²
Aboveground Floor Area: 38,937m², including:
Teaching Building: 8,907m²
Comprehensive Building: 12,363m²
Administration Building: 2,235m²
Dormitory: 4,980m²
Canteen: 4,415m²
Gymnasium: 3,722m²
Security Room: 141m²
Underground Floor Area: 2,174m²
Site Coverage: 17%
Design/Completion Time: 2007/2009
Architect: DONG Yi / DC Alliance Pte Ltd, Singapore
Photographer: DC Alliance Pte Ltd, Singapore
Client: Education Bureau of Jiangbei District, Ningbo

Cicheng Middle School has 60 classes of junior students, and the main teaching facilities include common teaching building, public teaching building, science and technology library, administration building, gymnasium, canteen, dormitory and other auxiliary facilities.

Master Plan
1. Structure of Space and Rhythm
With the design principle of "tradition with innovation, structure with rhythm", the master plan of the school can be concluded as "three sections, one axis, two belts, and four courtyards". To be specific, they are: three sections for three programmes: administration and service section, teaching section, and sports section.
One axis: the north-south axis of the school with the starting point at the school entrance
Two belts: one is the L-shaped "activity belt" at the school centre; the other is the natural "landscape belt" along the water across the school.
Four courtyards: two courtyards in teaching section, a living courtyard, and a circulation landscape courtyard.

Meanwhile, professionally the architects believe that the new school should have the following important features:
1). Multiple enchanting school environments, with which the school could meet educational, social, ecological, cultural and psychological needs.
2). The spaces, both interior and exterior, should be in human scale to give pleasing spatial experience.

3). Buildings in different sections should be easily recognisable, with identifying features to their own. In general, the buildings are simple, clear and elegant.
4). A harmonious relationship should be established among buildings, human beings and environments.

2. Programmes
Since the middle school has relatively complex programmes, the architects tried to reasonably arrange the different sections on the existing site. It is an east-west plot which is crossed by a north-south channel. The architects decided to set the three sections in an east-west direction, with the administration and service section and the teaching section on the two sides of the main road, and the teaching section and sports section separated by the channel. In this way, the different sections are arranged reasonably, in a clear and interconnected way.

The teaching section is no doubt the core of the school. Public teaching spaces such as classrooms, labs and library are integrated into a multi-purpose complex, contrasting with traditional introversive class units. The sunken plaza between the two parts becomes a lively activity centre for the whole school.

3. Architecture
For school architecture, there are strict requirements for space between buildings to avoid interference between each other. Meanwhile, as standard

Site Plan (Below):
1. School main access
2. Sunken plaza
3. Teaching Building
4. Teaching Building (Building #2)
5. Comprehensive Building (Building #5)
6. Gymnasium (Building #6)
7. Canteen
8. Dormitory (Building #4)
9. Administration Building (Building #3)
10. Vehicle parking
11. Bicycle parking
12. Basketball court
13. Volleyball court
14. Sports field (400m track)
15. School subsidiary access
16. Central plaza

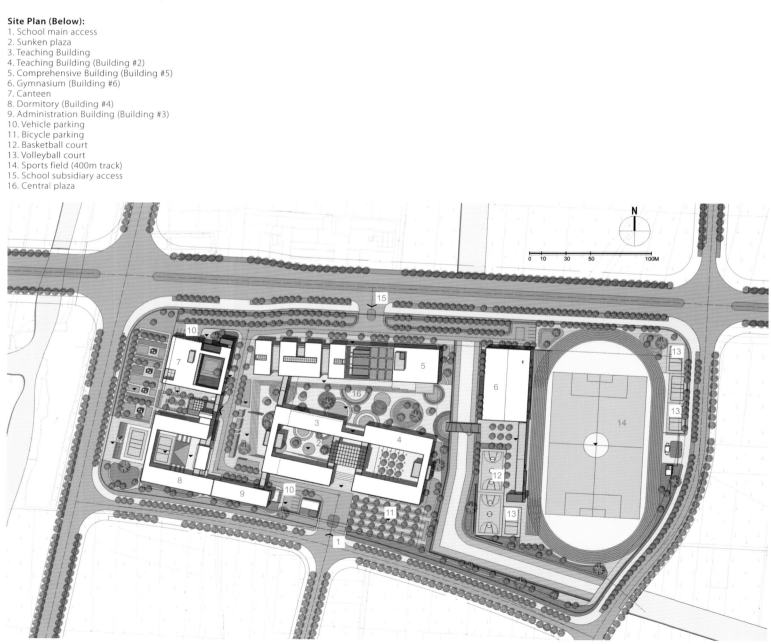

classrooms and labs, the room size and depth are specifically required. After learning these requirements, the architects established a balance that both guarantees the quietness of learning environments and creates comfortable scale and atmosphere. To be specific, administration building and students' dormitory are arranged on the south; canteen, comprehensive building and playground are set on the north, and the teaching section is put at the core of the school. In this way, the main urban roads are kept intact and the learning environments are well protected from noise.

4. Circulation and Escape

Circulation on the site is well planned to have separated routes and entrances for pedestrians and vehicles. A large bicycle parking lot is located at the main entrance on the south, and several small bicycle lots are arranged in the living section for the convenience of students. Entrance for the underground car park is arranged at the school centre, so cars won't be driven into the core area if not necessary. The entrance axis and core activity belt are the main areas for pedestrians. The ground floor of the comprehensive building is open to connect the pedestrian entrance on the east with the central plaza, with a circulation encircling the sports section.

Vehicles enter the school through the roads on the south and north, while pedestrians enter from the entrance on the road that encircles the lake.

Motor vehicles enter the underground car park through the entry at the east of the main school entrance. The total capacity of both aboveground and underground car park is 61, in accordance with the urban plan.

5. Landscape

In this project, landscape design plays an important role in creating the desired atmosphere for the whole school. The existing exterior spaces are re-organised into plazas, streets, courtyards and sky garden. With the extensive water feature, the public, semi-open and private spaces are all integrated into a unified landscape system. The boundary between interior and exterior is blurred, and there is no absolute exterior space or interior space; instead, they are all transitional spaces. The central plaza is proposed to be named after the Ci Lake from which the architects drew inspiration. It is a vital part in creating the unique learning environment.

Design Principles

1). Highlights on sharing and openness

a. The teaching complex: an independent micro-city structure with staircases between different levels as long as possible and decreasing openness as one goes upper and upper.

b. Structures built on stilts, multi-purpose circulation spaces, and three-dimensional resting places. Users will participate as much as possible.

1. Façade detail
2. Teaching building
3. Teaching building façade facing the street

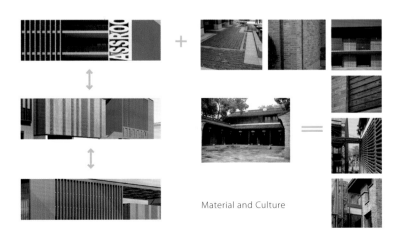

Material and Culture

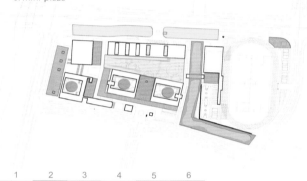

Circulation (Left):
1. Vehicle flow
2. Fire escape passage
3. Pedestrian flow
4. Parking aboveground
5. Access of parking underground
6. Main entrance
7. Subsidiary entrance
8. Urban roads

| 1 | 2 | 3 | 4 | 5 | 6 | 7 | 8 |

View Analysis:
1. Main view
2. Visual gallery

Landscape Logic:
1. Central plaza
2. Courtyard
3. Waterscape
4. Lawn
5. Concentrated greenery
6. Mini-plaza

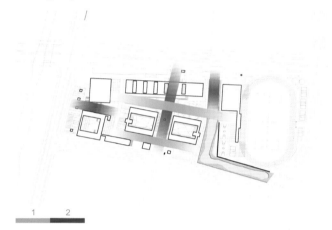

| 1 | 2 |

| 1 | 2 | 3 | 4 | 5 | 6 |

Structure and Dynamism

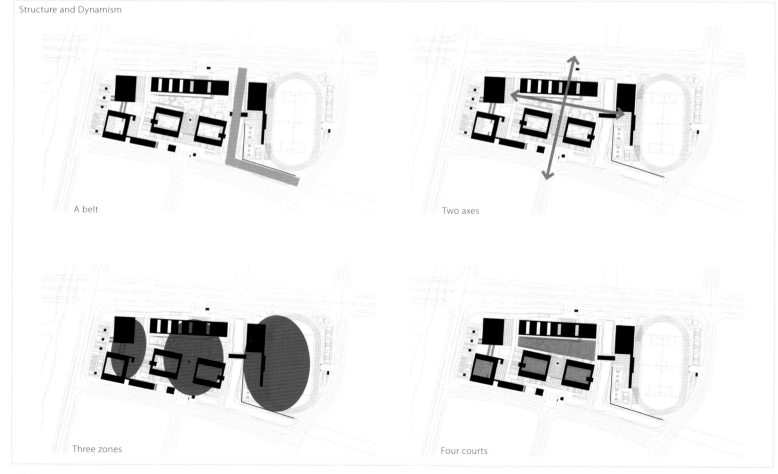

A belt

Two axes

Three zones

Four courts

c. Learning is possible everywhere. This is a symbol of transition from industrial society to information society in which information is acquired in a variety of ways.

2). Integration of modernity and locality

a. Architectural configuration: modern configuration + local materials

b. Spatial structure: modern space + local structural models

c. Spirit of space: modern functions + local culture

Architectural Design

1. Programmes

The project mainly consists of seven buildings: administration building, two teaching buildings that form a courtyard, comprehensive building that accommodates common classrooms, public classrooms, lecture hall and library, canteen, dormitory and playground. The teaching buildings are four-storey high, with a height of 3.9 metres, occupied by four grades independently, interconnected by galleries and connected with teacher's offices with staircase terraces. The comprehensive building is five-storey high, with a height of 3.9 metres, occupied by common classrooms on the ground floor and by the library, lecture hall and public classrooms on the upper floors. On the second floor, a corridor is connected with the teaching building. On the roof of the lecture hall, a terrace is designed for activities. The administration building is five-storey high, with a height of 3.6 metres, connected with the teaching building on the first floor. The canteen is three-storey high, with student's dining halls on the ground and first floor (floor height: 4.2 metres) and teacher's dining hall on the second floor (floor height: 3.9 metres); besides, a sky garden is located on the second floor facing the central plaza. The dormitory is five-storey high, with a height of 3.6 metres, with teacher's lodging on the south connected with the administration building. The two-storey playground is occupied by a swimming pool on the ground floor (floor height: 6 metres) and a basketball court on the first floor (floor height: 10 metres).

2. Spaces

The school is like a micro-city, with an open plan and a rich variety of spaces. It has to not only meet the needs of teaching and learning, but also provide multiple spaces for free communication. Therefore, the architects attached great importance in creating public spaces to reflect social changes. Closed walls are abandoned; roof terrace is created; architecture is built on stilts; spaces for learning and communication with different scales are purposefully arranged to encourage equal communication. The

Programmes (Right):
Three Zones:
1. Service zone
2. Teaching and administration zone
3. Sports zone
Architecture Layout:
1. Fengyu playground
2. Library
3. Lecture hall
4. Public classroom
5. Canteen
6. Bridge house
7. Teaching units
8. Sculpture
9. Tower at main entrance
10. Parents waiting area
11. Administration Building
12. Students' dormitory
and teachers' dormitory

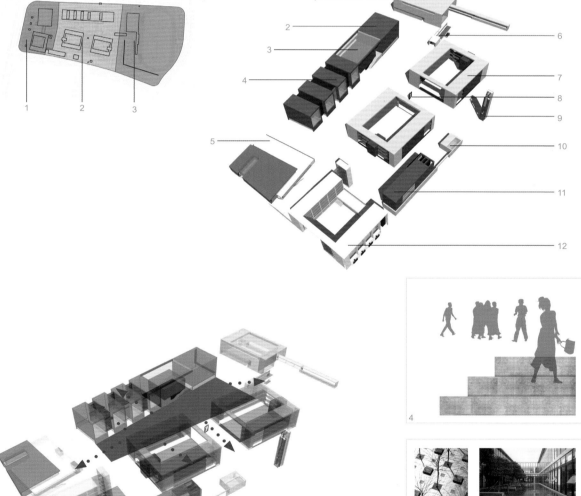

Dialogue and Space Interaction:
1. Central plaza
2. Stilted space
3. Courtyard
4. Steps
5. Spaces

architects believed that there shouldn't be a clear goal; instead, people could have different understanding and interpretation, and the users would endow the buildings with their own characteristics through use. The architecture should be flexible to cope with different needs, but it does not simply mean empty spaces ready for flexible use; rather, it should have the feature of – as the architects called it – multivalence, in terms of extensive possibility and efficiency. In the teaching section, with the open ground floor and sky garden, spaces feel like both interior and exterior so that you can't say whether you are inside a building or in between. The architecture is perfectly integrated with natural environment.

3. Elevation

Since it is the first educational project in the newly developed Cicheng Town, the client required the complex to be an iconic architecture for the town. The architects believed that architectural identity comes from uniqueness, clear configuration and intense contrast with the urban setting. In this project, the uniqueness lies in a cultural and ideological sense. With respect for traditional urban plans, spatial scales, quiet environment and local ideology of modesty, the architects combined modernity with locality in the architecture design, and resulted in the unique place in terms of spatial experience, visiting sequence, material and culture.

As for architectural configuration, modern and local features are both highlighted. The contemporary and simplistic buildings are endowed with a bit of traditional beauty, a style that is highly unique and enchanting. The buildings with different shapes create a rhythm that highlights the mass of the complex and its educational function. Paints, steel, glass, black bricks and timber are the main façade materials. With the limited elements, a piece of rhythmic "flowing music" is created on the façades.

4. Material and Culture

Requirements on tradition, locality, culture… With such a weight on the mind, the architects couldn't face the design relaxed and freely. Fortunately, in contemporary context, material could be a ready sally port. With white and grey paints combined with some timer, black bricks and steel, the modern and simplistic buildings are endowed with a somewhat reminiscent feel, silently bringing out an air of culture.

4. Central square
5. Landscape around teaching building
6. Teaching building view from basketball court

7. School entrance
8. Inner courtyard of teaching building
9. East view of teaching building along the river

9

SHENYANG NUMBER TWO HIGH SCHOOL, NORTH DISTRICT
Shenyang, Liaoning Province
LV Panfeng / New World Architecture Design Co., Ltd., Shenyang

Site Area: 158,700m²
Gross Floor Area: 87,000m²
Design/Completion Time: 2004-2005/2006
Architect: LV Panfeng / New World Architecture Design Co., Ltd., Shenyang
Design Team: ZHENG Min, ZENG Jie, LIU Na, LI Xinwei
Photographer: LV Panfeng
Client: Number Two High School
Greening Rate: 65%
Plot Ratio: 0.51
Building Height: 23.95m
Structure: Frame Structure

Number Two High School at North District is located at New District at the North of Shenyang, on the south bank of Pu River, with New Town Road on the south, South Pu Road on the north, and North Dili Street on the east. An architecture for 48 classes of high school students is sited on a plot of 158,700 square metres.

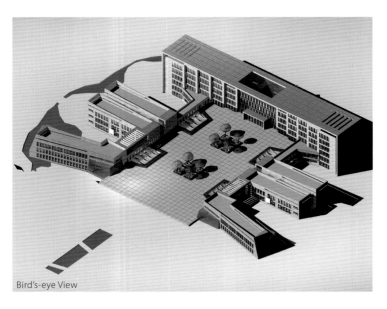
Bird's-eye View

The design principle of this project is to take advantage of the site and make some reasonable changes, illustrating the frozen music with plain notes. The surrounding natural environment is to be kept as much as possible.

The site is a sloping plot with the south end higher than the north. In the middle there is a terrace with a height difference of three to four metres, which is well adopted in the one-storey central library. The library connects the single buildings together, forming a two-storey circulation system linking interior spaces on different heights. Varied heights and interior/exterior spaces, as well as tens of existing trees, provide a beautiful environment for the teachers and students at Number Two High School.

Façades of the teaching building are made of 300mm-wide building blocks, either grey-painted or clad with grey stone. Fixed vertical louvres are adopted on façades of the stadium in order to reduce the penetrating sunshine for a better interior lighting effect.

In classrooms in the main teaching building, columns are arranged in a grid system of 9.0mX7.8m. The floors are made of high-tensile thin plates, with less weight and thickness than cast-in-situ ones, thus reducing project cost. The columns in the library are regularly distributed, and a special cross roof girder is adopted. A semi-exterior courtyard is designed in the centre of the library, which has a steel-structured roof with glass skylights to ensure natural lighting and ventilation for the semi-underground library.

2

Main Teaching Building Elevation:
1. Vestibule
2. Semi-basement library
3. Inner courtyard

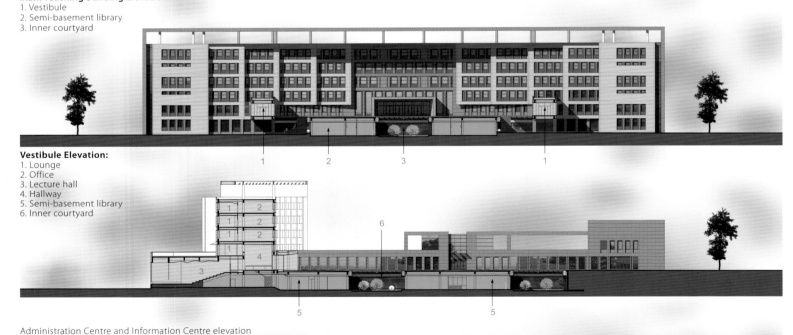

Vestibule Elevation:
1. Lounge
2. Office
3. Lecture hall
4. Hallway
5. Semi-basement library
6. Inner courtyard

Administration Centre and Information Centre elevation

1. Plaza at the main teaching building
2. Main teaching building

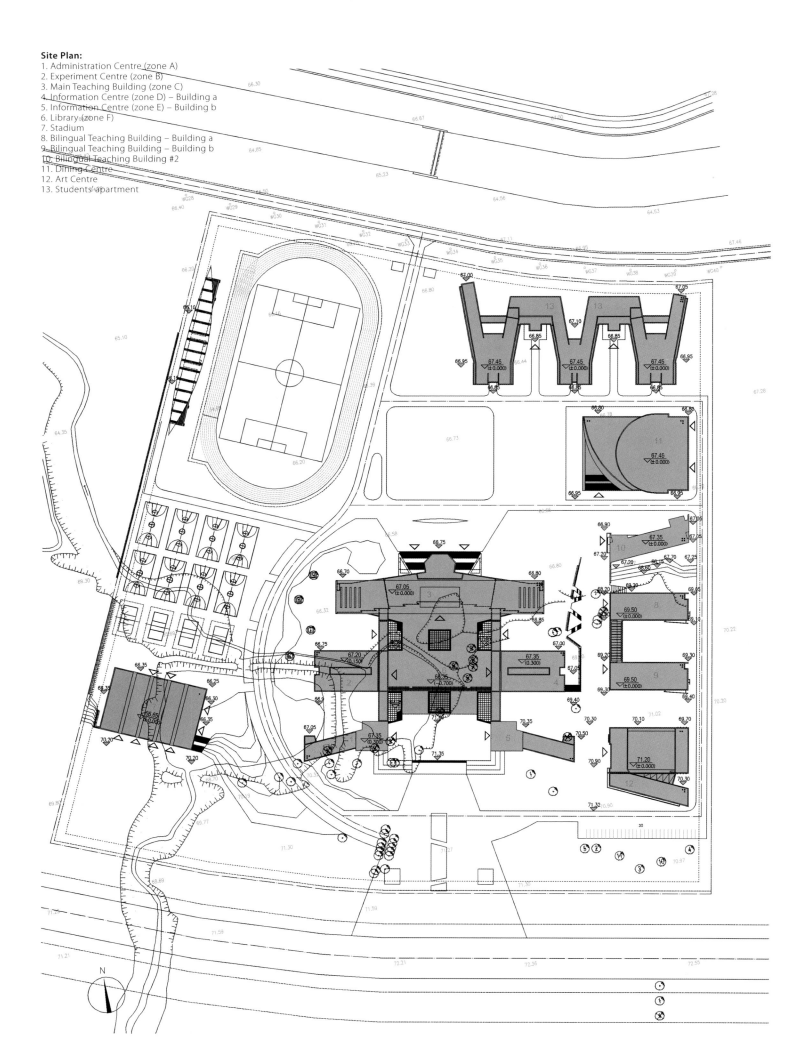

Site Plan:
1. Administration Centre (zone A)
2. Experiment Centre (zone B)
3. Main Teaching Building (zone C)
4. Information Centre (zone D) – Building a
5. Information Centre (zone E) – Building b
6. Library (zone F)
7. Stadium
8. Bilingual Teaching Building – Building a
9. Bilingual Teaching Building – Building b
10. Bilingual Teaching Building #2
11. Dining Centre
12. Art Centre
13. Students' apartment

3. Linking vestibule viewed from library roof
4. Vestibule in the integrated building
5. Detail of main teaching building

6. Integrated building courtyard
7. Existing tree preserved

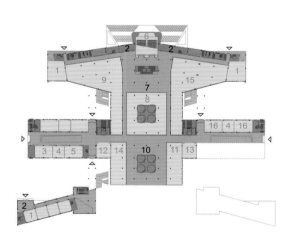

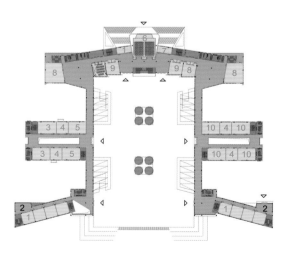

Main Teaching Building Ground Floor Plan:
1. Office
2. Lounge
3. Presentation room
4. Preparation room
5. Laboratory
6. Lecture hall
7. Internet hall
8. E-books reading room
9. Reading room
10. Exhibition room
11. Periodicals
12. Photocopy
13. Administration room
14. Teachers' reading room
15. Book storage
16. Computer room
17. Café

Main Teaching Building First Floor Plan:
1. Office
2. Lounge
3. Presentation room
4. Preparation room
5. Laboratory
6. Meeting room
7. Reception
8. Large classroom
9. Classroom
10. Computer room
11. Apartment

8. Back of the main teaching building
9. Bilingual teaching building #C
10. Slope greening
11. Main façade of bilingual building
12. School view

13

13. Experiment building
14. School landscape
15. View of experiment building from interior
16, 17. Interior of experiment building
18. Gymnasium
19. Art Centre
20. East façade

14

15

16

17

Stadium Ground Floor Plan:
1. Equipment storage
2. Ping-pang
3. Storage

Stadium First Floor Plan:
1. Auditorium with a capacity of 1,030
2. Void

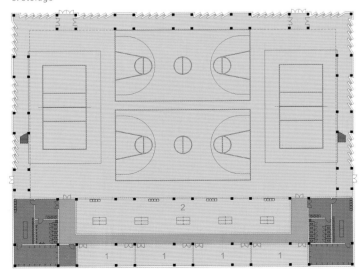

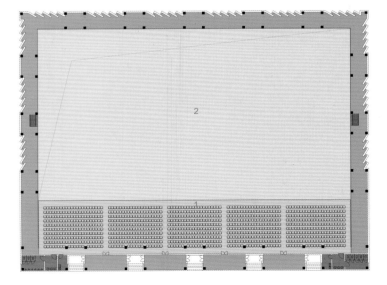

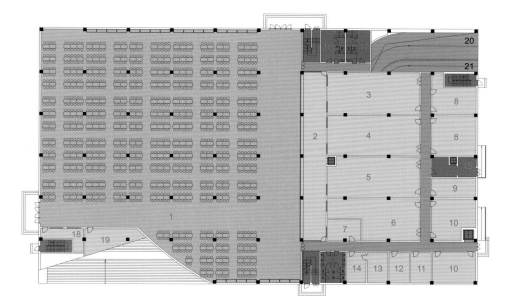

Dining Centre Ground Floor Plan:
1. Students' canteen with a capacity of 1,348
2. Preparation room
3. Pastry preparation
4. Staple food preparation
5. Subsidiary food fining-off and cooking
6. Subsidiary food preliminary preparation
7. Cooked food
8. Staple food storage
9. Cold storage
10. Subsidiary food storage
11. Drinks storage
12. Spices storage
13. Disinfection room
14. Dishwashing
15. Cleaning room
16. Female locker room and lounge
17. Male locker room and lounge
18. Card selling
19. Clearing
20. Vehicle ramp
21. Bicycle ramp

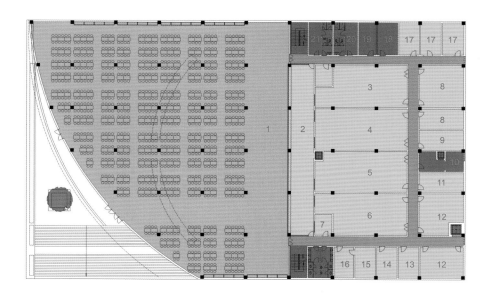

Dining Centre First Floor Plan:
1. Students' canteen with a capacity of 1,136
2. Preparation room
3. Subsidiary food preparation for the Huis
4. Staple food preparation
5. Subsidiary food fining-off and cooking
6. Subsidiary food preliminary preparation
7. Cooked food
8. Staple food storage
9. Spices storage
10. Cleaning room
11. Cold storage
12. Subsidiary food storage
13. Tableware storage
14. Drinks storage
15. Disinfection room
16. Dishwashing
17. Office
18. Male lounge
19. Female lounge
20. Female locker room
21. Male locker room

21. Surrounding landscape
    of student dormitory
22. Student dormitory

**Student Dormitory Ground Floor Plan
(Gross Floor Area: 24,845m²):**
1. Dorm
2. Individual study room
3. Terrace
4. Hot water/cleaning

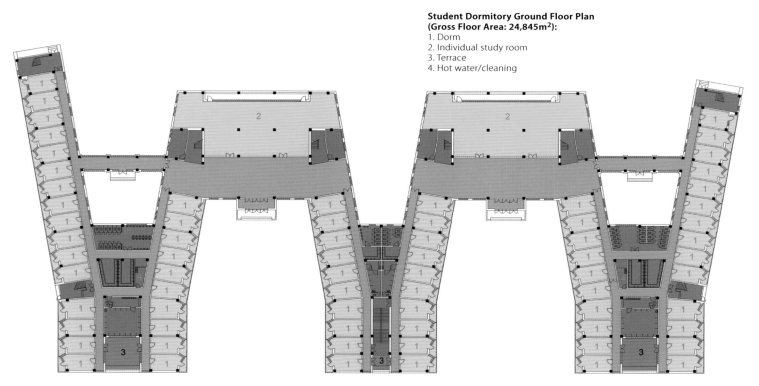

WEST DISTRICT SENIOR MIDDLE SCHOOL IN BAYAN NUR
Bayan Nur, Inner Mongolia
China Architecture Design & Research Group

Site Area: 113,220m²
Gross Floor Area: 75,922m²
Design/Completion Time: 2011
Architect: China Architecture Design & Research Group
Design Team: CAO Xiaoxin, SHEN Xiaolei, YU Hao
Photographer: ZHANG Guangyuan

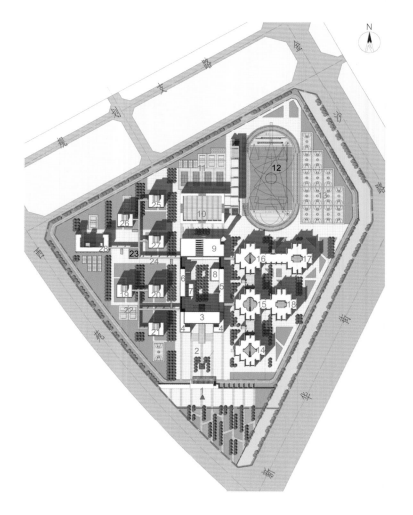

The project starts from criticising school architecture stereotypes. Slab-type architecture used to be conventional buildings for schools in China. At present, national regulations on primary and middle school design and administration put emphasis on basic functions of school, especially on teaching. As for other programmes apart from teaching, there is no particular demand. However, traditional stereotypes have dominated school design, resulting in the ignorance of human experience and multi-functional spaces.

In this project, the architects attached great importance to the teaching building, trying to find a new approach. After a research on teaching functions, they set five independent yet interrelated sections: three sections for grade one, two and three respectively, lab section, and public teaching function. Furthermore, they designed five courtyards according to five kinds of behaviours, including meditation courtyard, wander courtyard, appreciation courtyard and performance courtyard. Through deformation of simple rectangular courts, the architects enriched the five kinds of school life in a spatial and montage approach.

Site Plan (Left):

1. Main entrance	15. Teaching Building #2
2. Front plaza	16. Teaching Building #3
3. Office Building	17. Laboratory #1
4. Library	18. Laboratory #2
5. School History Pavilion	19. Male students' dormitory #1
6. Group Activity Building	20. Male students' dormitory #2
7. Conference Office Building	21. Male students' dormitory #3
8. Conference Building	22. Bathroom
9. Canteen	23. Hot water
10. Gymnasium	24. Vestibule built on stilts
11. Tennis court	25. Female students' dormitory #1
12. Sports field	26. Female students' dormitory #2
13. Basketball court	27. Female students' dormitory #3
14. Teaching Building #1	28. Teachers' dormitory

2

The teaching building was built on stilts on the ground floor in order to leave the outside space open and fluid. In this way, areas on the ground floor are connected, giving more freedom for wander.

Good architecture is like good movies – they are composed of many memorable fragments. The design of the middle school, particularly the five courtyards in the teaching building, as an attempt to find new approaches to school design, aims to leave beautiful memories for its users – beautiful stories that happened in the various spaces.

1. Entrance
2. Panoramic view of the main building

A. Programmes Topology:
1. Sports
2. Dormitory
3. Canteen
4. Library and office
5. Front plaza
6. Teaching

B. Direction and Daylight: South Facing for Maximum Daylight

C. Area Allocation:
1. Gymnasium: 4,000
2. Dormitory: 22,000
3. Canteen: 4,000
4. Library: 5,800; Office: 5,000
5. Teaching: 29,000

D. Roads: Surrounding Roads

E.Entrance and Vehicle Circulation
1. Entrance
2. Main entrance

F. Relationship among Zones:
1. Sports
2. Dormitory
3. Public service
4. Teaching

G. Greenery and Landscape:
Surrounding greenery
1. Urban public greenery
2. Green belts

H. Green Area within Site: Green Area and Sports Field

I. Greenery and Architecture Integrated: Greenery between Buildings

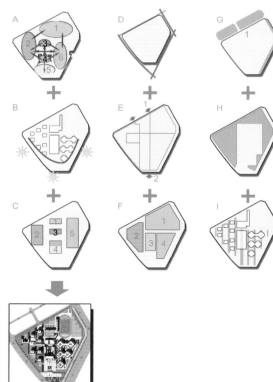

3. Aerial view of the main building
4. Main building plaza
5. A glimpse of the plaza

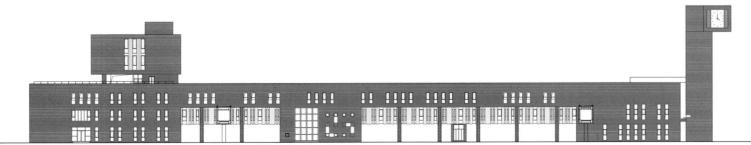

Main Building Elevations

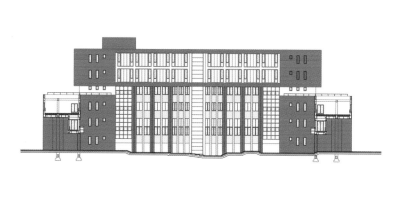

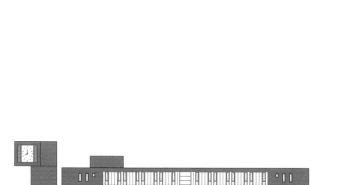

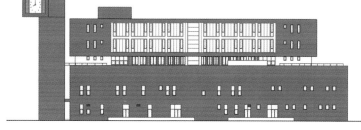

Main Building Elevations

6. Close-up of main building
7. Bell tower
8. Corridor

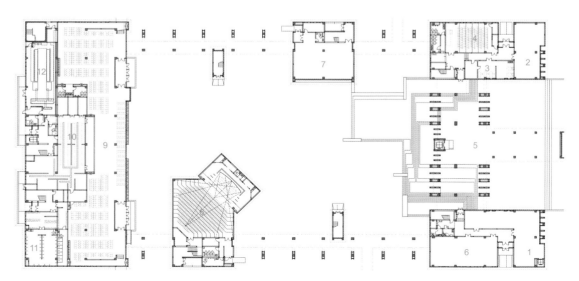

**Main Building
Ground Floor Plan:**
1. Book storage
2. Archives
3. Infirmary
4. Conference room
5. Hall
6. Distance learning classroom
7. School supermarket
8. Conference room
   (projection)
9. Dining area
10. Kitchen
11. Male bathroom
12. Electric room

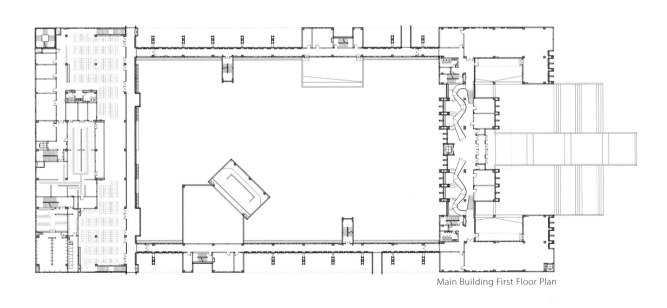

Main Building First Floor Plan

155

9. Teaching building
10. Teaching building landscape
11. Staircase landing

Teaching Building North Elevation

Teaching Building East Elevation

Teaching Building Section

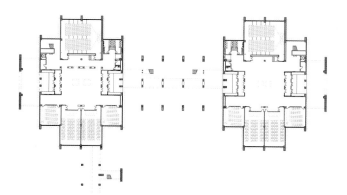

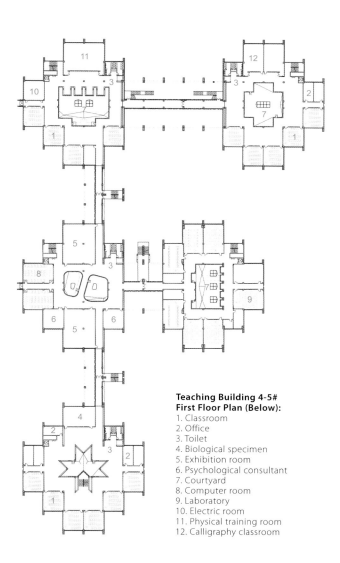

**Teaching Building 4-5#
First Floor Plan (Below):**
1. Classroom
2. Office
3. Toilet
4. Biological specimen
5. Exhibition room
6. Psychological consultant
7. Courtyard
8. Computer room
9. Laboratory
10. Electric room
11. Physical training room
12. Calligraphy classroom

12. Dormitory buildings surrounded with landscape
13. Perspective of dormitory buildings

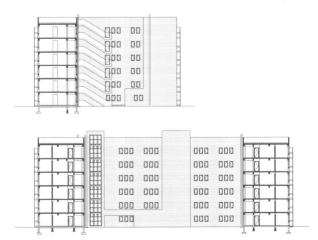

Teachers' Dormitory Sections

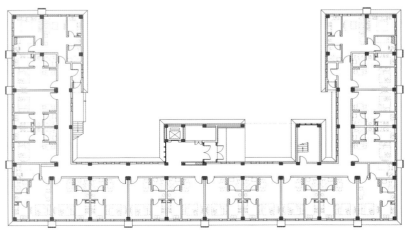

Teachers' Dormitory Ground Floor Plan

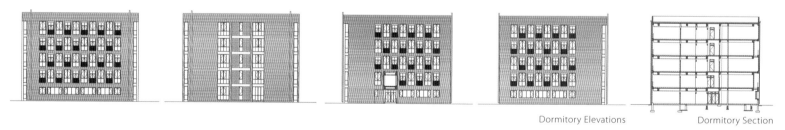

Dormitory Elevations

Dormitory Section

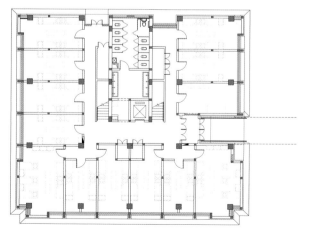

Students' Dormitory Ground Floor Plan

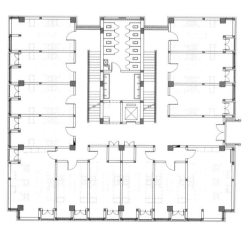

Students' Dormitory First Floor Plan

159

PRIMARY SCHOOL AT C09 PLOT, SOUTHSTAR COMMUNITY, QIANJIANG NEW TOWN

Hangzhou, Zhejiang Province
Beijing Institute of Architectural Design (BIAD)

Site Area: 17,346m²
Gross Floor Area: 18,436m²
Design/Completion Time: 2007-2009/2009
Architect: Beijing Institute of Architectural Design (BIAD)
Design Team: LI Chengde, WANG Shuzhan, SUN Xiaoming, YUAN Lipu, ZHENG Zhenzhen, LIU Rong, HAN Zhaoqiang, ZENG Yuan, SHEN Jie, LI Zhenyu
Photographer: YANG Chaoying

The project of this primary school at C09 Plot, SouthStar Community, Qianjiang New Town is mainly challenged by two disadvantageous site conditions: a limited site area and a slanting lot. The architects from BIAD found an appropriate solution, successfully arranging programmes such as the main teaching building, a sports field, and an art centre in a clear plan, creating easy circulation in both interior and exterior.

Space

Unlike traditional primary schools which only have the basic school functions and no more, the design of this primary school particularly made some exploration about "space". Since Hangzhou has a humid and hot climate, the architects created many semi-outdoor circulation spaces that are good at rain-proofing and ventilation. Green inner courtyards and open verandas are interconnected to organise main programmes. In this way, natural lighting and ventilation is achieved, making the architecture open and transparent. The courtyards resemble traditional Chinese gardens, which not only provide ever-changing sceneries but also reveal a strong oriental feature. Meanwhile, children are given more chances to be close to nature, and thus freed from overprotection in the teaching building.

The colonnade, main entrance, vestibule, school culture hall, arc staircase, main corridor, and training centre constitute the main axis of the teaching building, organising the different programmes in good order. These spaces perfectly reveal the aesthetics of order in traditional Chinese architecture. Moreover, typical Chinese patterns and icons appear in the interiors; in the colonnade the column bases are derived from Chinese drum-shaped bearing stone; Chinese traditional lattice is used extensively in both interior and exterior; Chinese flowering crabapple pattern is adopted in the school culture hall. All in all, the architects tried to incorporate Chinese imagery into the architecture in a contemporary way, drawing students closer to

traditional Chinese culture in their daily life.

Various spaces are created for children who, apart from routine classrooms, can enjoy an interesting school life. The ceremonial school culture hall looks dignified and somber; the zigzagging corridor beside the classrooms is intimate and welcoming; the 6-metre-wide porch before the classroom is bright and open; the roof terrace is good for playing, exposing to or taking shelter from the rain; the veranda at the perimeter of the atrium is playful and interesting; the green inner courtyards are quiet and cosy. The various space types provide children with multiple opportunities for beautiful stories and a memorable childhood.

Construction

With an extremely limited budget, the architecture is austere in material, both interior and exterior. However, following the principle of "raw material, delicate detail", the architects successfully improved the quality of construction.

Grey bricks were selected for the façade to give out a hint of traditional architecture, but were adopted in a new way. The bricks were layered with a 45-degree angle, differing from conventional horizontal brick construction. The special pattern formed on the façade enlivens the atmosphere of the school. Dark, intermediate, and light grey bricks are constructed with a proportion of 7:2:1. Dark grey is the basic tone, while the other two become lively elements on the façade.

Traditional lattice is used throughout the building as a symbol of Chinese architecture, for example, in the main entrance curtain wall, the open suspended ceiling, and openings on the ceiling and side walls. The lattice in wood colour, together with the light yellow-painted ceiling, contrasts

1. Façade close-up view
2. Main façade
3. Façade detail
4. School entrance

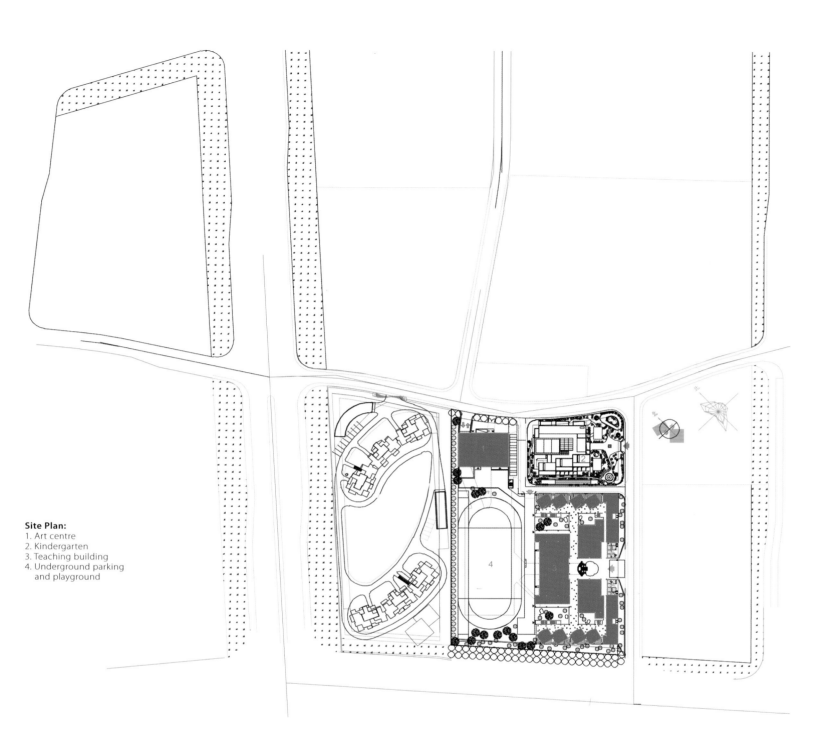

Site Plan:
1. Art centre
2. Kindergarten
3. Teaching building
4. Underground parking
   and playground

5. Teaching building view
   from playground
6. Inner courtyard
7. Staircase

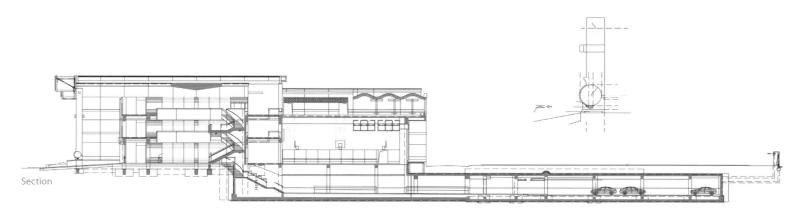

Section

164

with the grey façade, creating an atmosphere full of Chinese flavour while highlighting the warm texture of the building.

Columns and railings are constructed with the technique called "concrete chip-axe". Compared with real stone paving, this traditional technique creates a similar effect; it is cost-effective, and brings out the aesthetics of simplicity. Moreover, it is more flexible in nodes and articulation details.

The principle of "raw material, delicate detail" is a direct challenge to the currently popular mode of "luxury material, raw craftsmanship". Many delicate construction techniques in Chinese ancient architecture have been lost in the process of rapid development of the country. In this project, it was difficult to carry out such a principle for the deficiency of constructors' skills, the time limit... Nonetheless, at present when budget for educational projects is still low, it is an efficient way to improve architectural quality.

The architectural design for this primary school breaks the stereotype of educational architecture (plain spaces, atmosphere all in the same key, lack of delicate details...). Currently the country is promoting transformation in fundamental education, and this project is just a good example of transformation, in the perspective of architecture.

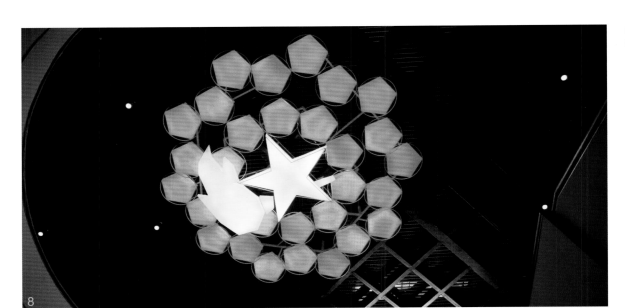

8. Special light: Sparkling Star
9. Lobby
10. Typical classroom

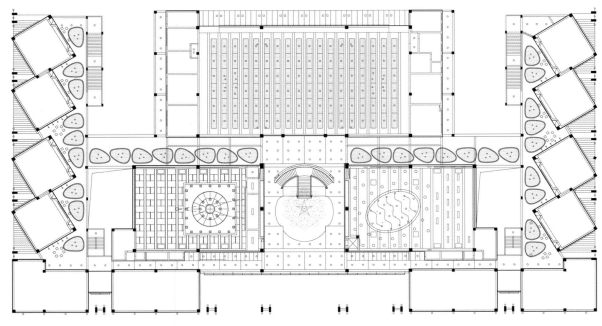

Outdoor Ceiling Plan with Lights

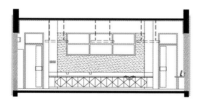
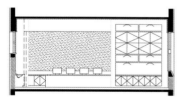
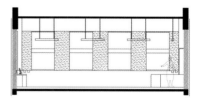
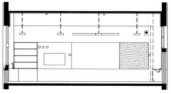

Classroom Sections

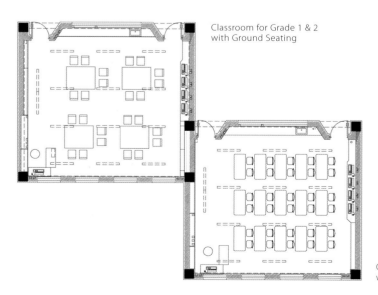

Classroom for Grade 1 & 2
with Ground Seating

Classroom for Grade 3 to 6
with Typical Seating

Ground Floor Plan (Right):
1. Main Entrance
2. Lobby
3. Office
4. Multi-functional training hall
5. Restroom
6. Secondary entrance
7. Courtyard sculpture
8. Library mezzanine floor

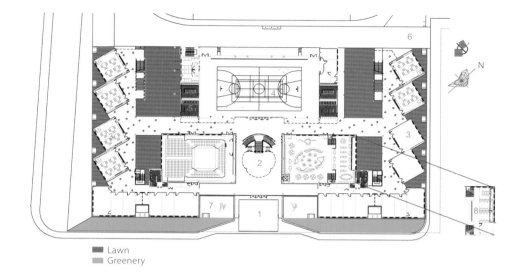

■ Lawn
■ Greenery

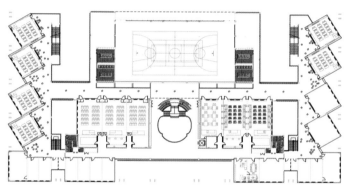

First Floor Plan

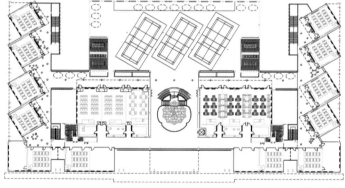

Second Floor Plan

11. Lecture hall
12. Multi-functional training hall

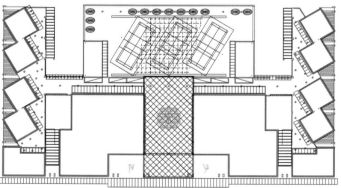

Roof Plan

EXPERIMENTAL PRIMARY SCHOOL & KINDERGARTEN, SUZHO

Suzhou, Jiangsu Province
9-Town Design Studio for Urban Architecture, Shanghai

Site Area: 52,170m²
Gross Floor Area: 64,165m²
Design/Completion Time: 2008/2010
Architect: 9-Town Design Studio for Urban Architecture, Shanghai
Design Team: YU Lei, HUANG Zhiqiang, XU Tian,
LI Lingyun, DENG Hongfeng, WANG Xiao, GUO Xing, QIN Feng
Collaborator: 9-Town Design Studio for Urban Architecture, Suzhou
Photographer: YAO Li
Client: Experimental Primary School, Suzhou

The Experimental Primary School, Suzhou has a history of 100 years. In 2008 due to the redevelopment of the old town, the City Government decided to relocate the primary school and its affiliated kindergarten. Construction on the new site is scheduled to accommodate 60 classes for the primary school and 18 classes for the kindergarten. Because the site is located at the urban centre, the architects are confronted with a series of problems: the limitation of site area, a high demand for floor area, the lack of event and green spaces, etc.

With the above-mentioned problems in mind, the architects designed the new school architecture as a complex, with different programme spaces united by a linking system. In this way, spaces both above and under ground are fully utilised, and different rooms, event spaces and circulation are three-dimensionally organised. The new school complex is an integral architecture with several sections including – sequentially from the north entrance – administration and public section, tutoring section and teaching section. Buildings of the three sections form several courtyards in a systematic "six horizontal plus three vertical cross-line" structure. The buildings were built on stilts as much as possible, leaving the ground floor as linking joints between courtyards in the tutoring and teaching section. In this way, the linking courtyards become the main axis of the public space in the school while tops of the classrooms on the lower floors become mid-air playgrounds which are connected with main roads. The intensification of space utility solves the conflict between the limited site and lack of event space.

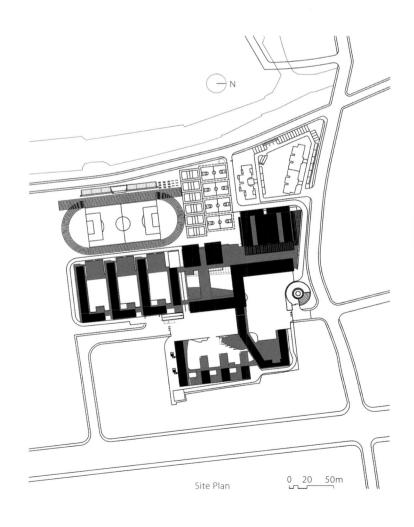

Site Plan

0 20 50m

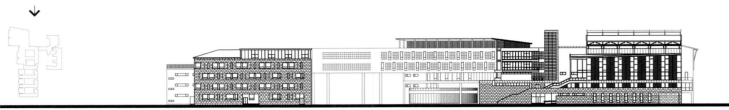

North Elevation of Primary School and Kindergarten

Elevation

1. Play space in the kindergarten
2. North façade of primary school and kindergarten and entrance square

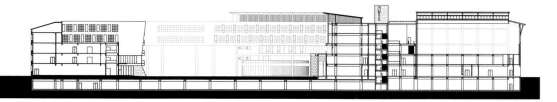

Primary School and Kindergarten Sections

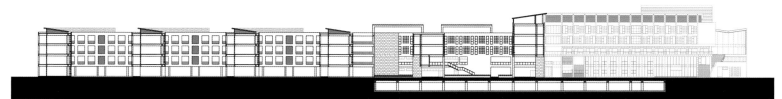

6

Façades of the architecture feature grey metal pitched roofs, beige stone and red bricks. The classic three-colour scheme becomes striking characteristics of the school. The pitched roofs characterise the enclosed public courtyards and contribute to the dynamic rise and fall of the architectural silhouette. The beige dry-fasten stone is used mainly on lower levels and façades facing the city to highlight the public and solemn character of the school. The in-between red bricks continue the tradition and history of the school. Thanks to the friendly texture of materials and the ternary composition of the façades, the vast complex won't feel depressing and suits well with children in scale.

3. Main entrance to the kindergarten
4. Main entrance square
5. Teaching building courtyard
6. Stilted teaching building, with a winding pavement linking all the courtyards

7

East Elevation

West Elevation

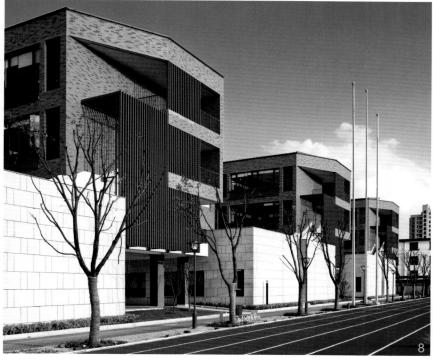

7. East stone façade of
   the primary school in a warm tone
8. West façade
9. South façade of the kindergarten

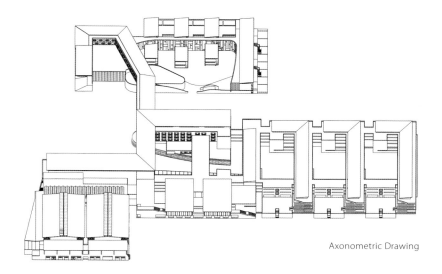

Axonometric Drawing

South Elevation

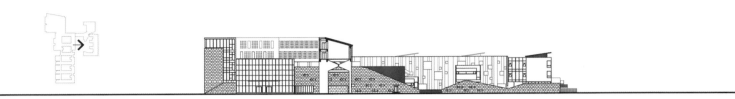

West Elevation of Kindergarten

10. Music & Sports facility in the kindergarten
11. Play space in the kindergarten
12. West façade of the kindergarten

13

13. Interior view of the Music and Sports facility
14. Indoor playground
15. Lecture hall

14

15

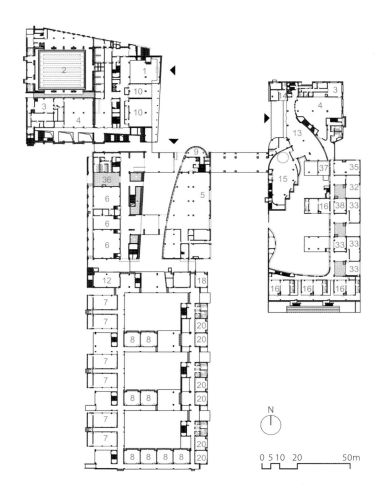

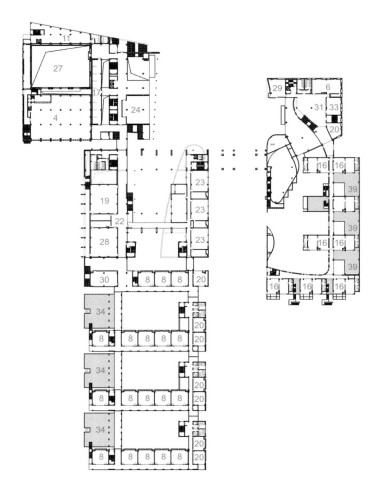

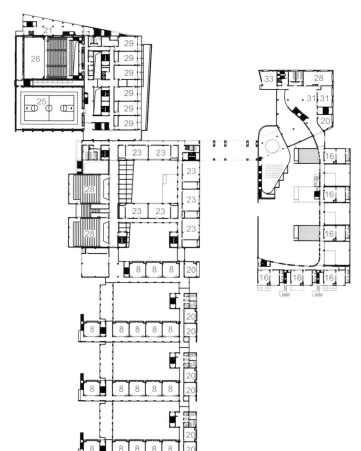

N

0 5 10 20   50m

Ground Floor Plan (Left Above),
First Floor Plan (Above)
and Second Floor Plan (Left):
1. Administration Building hall
2. Indoor pool
3. Kitchen
4. Students restaurant
5. Library
6. Dance classroom
7. Computer classroom
8. Classroom
9. Fire fighting control
10. Reception
11. General affairs
12. Plant room
13. Kindergarten hall
14. Morning checkout
15. Music & sport room
16. Activity room/bedroom
17. Exhibition room
18. Infirmary
19. Conference room
20. Teachers office
21. Lounge
22. Multimedia gallery
23. Auxiliary classroom
24. Teachers activity room
25. Playground
26. Lecture hall
27. Void
28. Multimedia classroom
29. Music classroom
30. Broadcasting room
31. Children library
32. Science & Discover room
33. Special classroom
34. Roof terrace
35. Meng pedagogy classroom
36. Courtyard
37. Sports room
38. Storeroom
39. Special outdoor play field

16. Open reading room on the second
 floor atrium of the kindergarten

ETHNIC PRIMARY SCHOOL IN XIAOQUAN TOWN
Deyang City, Sichuan Province
HUA Li / TAO (Trace Architecture Office)

Site Area: 16,826m²
Gross Floor Area: 8,900m²
Structure: Reinforced concrete frame
Use: Classrooms, multi-purpose rooms,
office, student dormitory, dining hall, etc.
Design/Completion Time: 2008-2009/2009-2010
Architect: HUA Li/TAO (Trace Architecture Office)
Design Team: ZHU Zhiyuan, JIANG Nan, LI Guofa, KONG Desheng
Photographer: YAO Li, JIANG Nan
Contractor: Huaxiluyi Construction Co., Ltd., Sichuan
Sponsors: Red Cross Society, Taicang, Jiangsu; Liuzu Buddhism Temple Charity, Sihui, Guangdong; Tsinghua & HKCU MBA Group; Peking University HSBC School of Business PE Fund; Qiaoai Organisation; Sichuan Society for Promotion of the Guangcai Programme

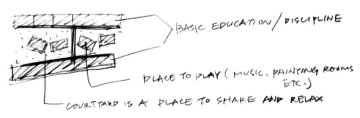

Background

The May 12th Earthquake destroyed the original Ethnic Primary School in Jingyang District, Deyang. Reconstruction was urgently in need. Xiaoquan town, with a population of about 40 thousand, is located on the northwest of Deyang, and is one of the most seriously destroyed areas in the earthquake. The reconstruction project includes a teaching building with 18 classrooms, multi-purpose rooms, student dormitory and dining hall, with a total floor area of more than 8,800 square metres.

The design begins on June 2008 when the architects came to Xiaoquan Town for site investigation. Due to the devastating earthquake, the buildings in the town completely collapsed or broke to be dilapidated.

The common height of local architecture is two to four storeys, and streets are five to six metres wide, with twisting plans that are typical characteristics of historic towns. The original elementary school destroyed in the earthquake has been demolished, and a new site has been chosen on a nearby old street. The site area is a little smaller than the original, but is had to accommodate more students (about 900), among whom many are children of the farmers who come to town for work. Therefore, student dormitory and dining hall are necessary on the limited site. Temporary houses were built on the west of the site for junior high school students, which were scheduled to be demolished after the completion of the elementary school.

Strategy

Before going to the site, the architects had been thinking for strategies. For disaster areas, reconstruction is a kind of development by leaps and bounds because capital, technology and awareness all come at once. Steps of local modernisation would speed up. Then, what should be the right attitude towards local traditions? Should the area take an altogether new look, or should it retain the memory of past space and life? Are workers, materials and building techniques transported from another area liable to make local characteristics disappear? Would local people positively join in the reconstruction, or just passively accept the result? Would local architecture industry make some progress or just stand by? In addition, in reconstruction efficiency is always urgently in need, and thus architectural industrialisation and standardisation easily become the mainstream. Would it lead to stereotyped buildings lacking of diversity, just like the case in Tangshan earthquake?

The fund for reconstruction of the Ethnic Elementary School came from different sponsors from various regions, who agreed to let the Education Bureau of Jingyang District handle the project. Therefore, according to local conventions, local contractors would be involved. Meanwhile, the new master plan of the town highlights the historical characteristics of

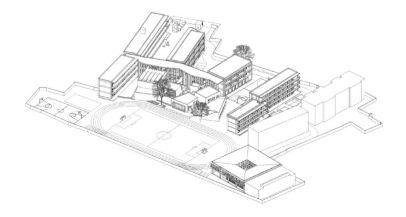

Overall Axonometric Drawing

1, 2. Street: recalling the memory of urban space in old Xiaoquan Town

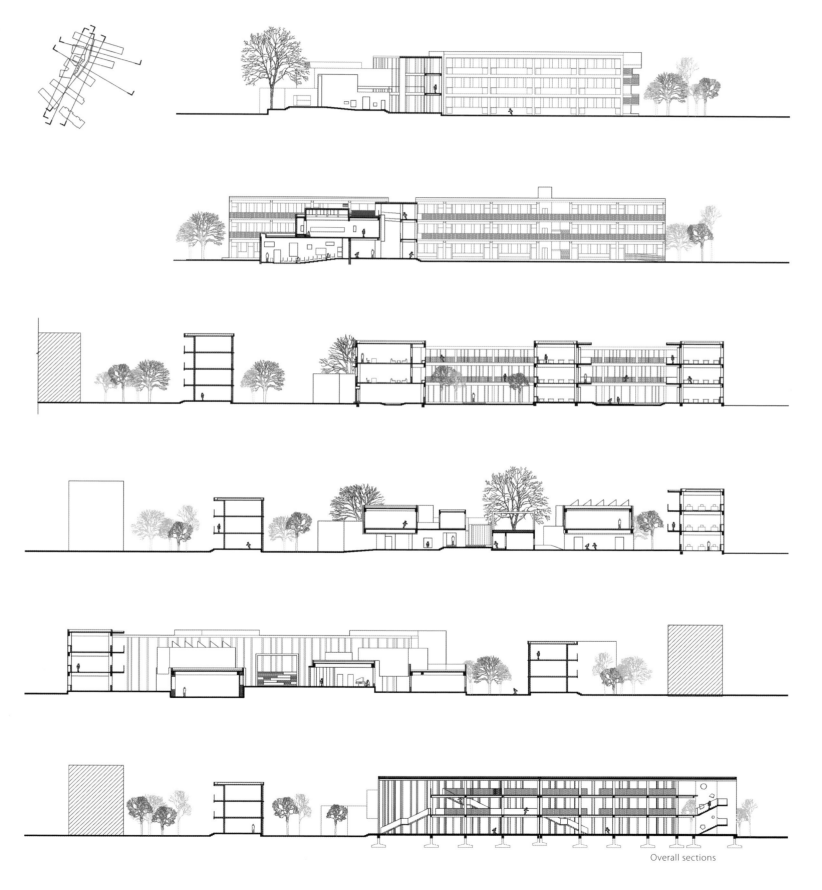

Overall sections

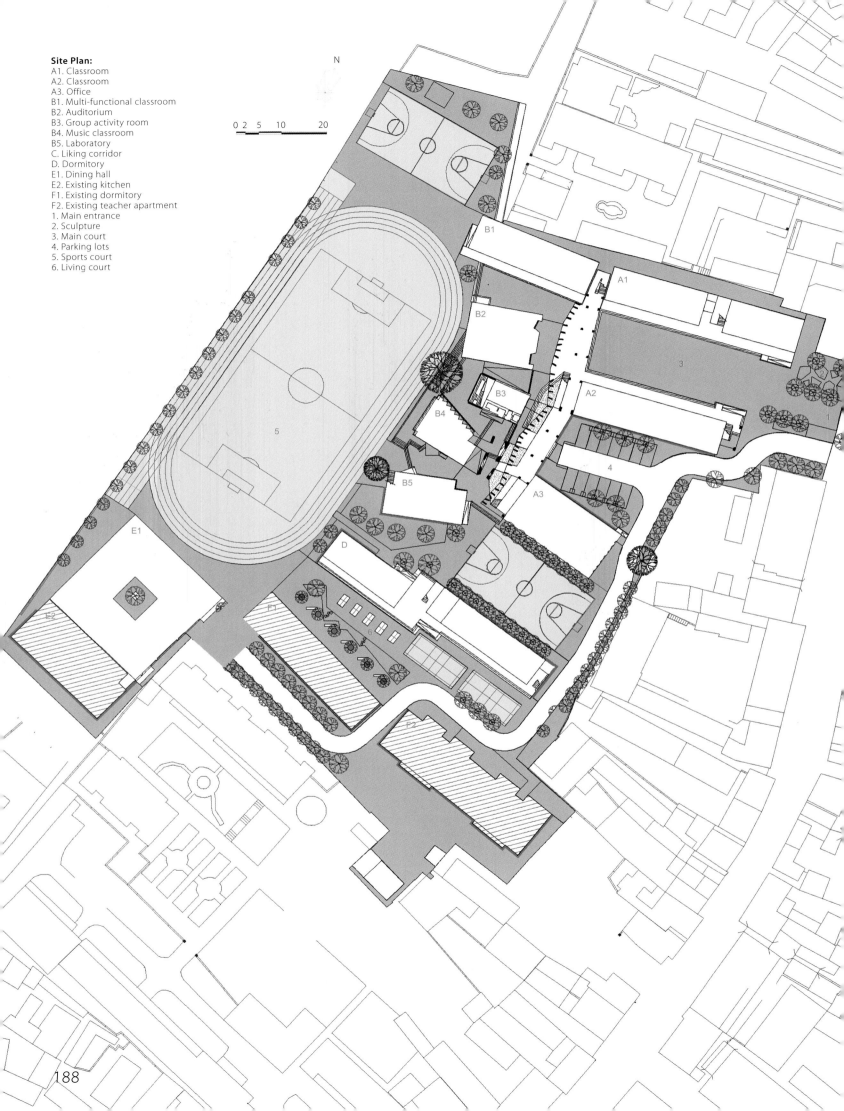

Site Plan:
A1. Classroom
A2. Classroom
A3. Office
B1. Multi-functional classroom
B2. Auditorium
B3. Group activity room
B4. Music classroom
B5. Laboratory
C. Liking corridor
D. Dormitory
E1. Dining hall
E2. Existing kitchen
F1. Existing dormitory
F2. Existing teacher apartment
1. Main entrance
2. Sculpture
3. Main court
4. Parking lots
5. Sports court
6. Living court

N

0 2 5 10   20

the old town. These conditions drive the architects to think about the interrelationship between the project and the region. Besides, without any unreasonable governmental deadline, the architects needn't sacrifice quality for efficiency.

The strategies for the project are based on two aspects: space and construction.

Space

In traditional schools, plans are set for the convenience of administration because there are always a large number of students and a rather small number of teachers, leading to prison-like spaces. Of course this is due to the limited budget, and this elementary school is no exception. In the project, concerning the layout the architects tried to keep children's perspective in mind, creating various, scattered and interesting spaces to encourage communication and multiplex activities between students, because after all, children are the main body of a school. The school is divided into three sectors: classrooms (Order Sector), multi-purpose rooms (Interest Sector), and outdoor ground (Relaxing Sector), offering different spaces for various activities.

Schools, as a kind of social space, should be conceived with particular local history. The architects are not interested in new types of memorial architecture. Instead, they conceive the school not as an architecture, but as a mini-city, which contains a micro society of students and teachers. In this sense, many spaces that belong to urban environment are created, such as streets, squares, courtyards and steps. The diverse spaces not only provide the pupils with different playing corners and interesting spaces for experience, arousing their curiosity and imagination when having fun, but also echo with the urban space of the town before earthquake in terms of scale and form. In this way, memory of the old town space is preserved, where the natural space complexity would give individuals more choices. Crude, overwritten reconstruction that totally demolishes the original urban space system is definitely not preferred. Sometimes it would be another disaster for people and their memory, psychologically.

The main body is located at the east part of the site, near the school gate on the old street. On the west is the sports field, where temporary houses for junior high school are built. Such an arrangement effectively protects students in class from noises of construction. On the south the new and existing dormitories form a new living courtyard, while on the southwest corner the dining hall is connected to the existing kitchen.

The main body consists of three parts: on the east are teaching building and office building; on the west are a computer classroom, a language teaching classroom, an amphitheatre, an art classroom, an activity room, a playing

gallery, a music classroom, two labs and their preparation rooms, etc. A vestibule (south-north, slightly twisting) between the east and west part connects all the programmes, which the architects called "spine". The spine acts for circulation, communication, ventilation and sun shade as well.

The teaching building and office building on the east are three-storey high, appropriate for children (buildings too high would be depressing), and the courtyard in between open to the main entrance of the school is easy for escape. Meanwhile, it acts as a solemn space for formal activities such as flag-rising ceremony and body exercise.

The multi-purpose classrooms on the west with different heights look like a micro city, with streets, steps, eaves gallery and courtyards, acting as a transitional area between the teaching building and sports field. The roof terrace further extends the usable outdoor spaces.

Two existing trees are preserved. A big Gleditsia sinensis nearly 20 metres high becomes the focal landscape facing the courtyard and steps. The steps act as a path connecting the teaching building and playground, and as a place for activities such as games, reading, photo-taking, and match-watching. Under the steps is the activity room, to the south of which a playing gallery is located containing several corners with different scales. The skylight connects the outer steps with the space where various activities

3. Model, 1:150

4

such as doing homework, kicking shuttlecocks and playing hide-and-seek take place. The children love this space and call it the "stone house".

The eaves gallery between the amphitheatre and playground has well-proportioned openings on the thick wall which are treated as alcoves as a kind of playing furniture for the children. In this way, the gallery is not only for circulation, and the openings create enchanting light and shadow effect in the interior.

The central spine is a vestibule connecting all the programmes. The side that faces the playground uses continuous concrete columns, creating a three-storey-high gallery space. The columns protect the space from the western sunlight and create an interesting light and shadow effect, enriching the visual experience. Three straight staircases connect different storeys, and several air-bridges link the art classroom, lab, steps and roof garden. On the ground floor, a long pool is designed between the columns and the staircases, effectively enlivening the space. Watching the fishes swimming in the pool is one of the favourite activities for the children.

A library occupies the ground floor of the teaching building. The south-facing slender windows are deeply embedded into the wall in order to protect the room from the sun and to avoid accidental ball crushing from the playground. Inside the library there are quiet reading corners.

In designing the dining hall, ventilation and lighting are considered as two keys. The architects decide to make it a square plan with an inner courtyard,

4. Bird's-eye view of multi-purpose classrooms
5. Big steps
6. Between school and sports field
7. View to the roof

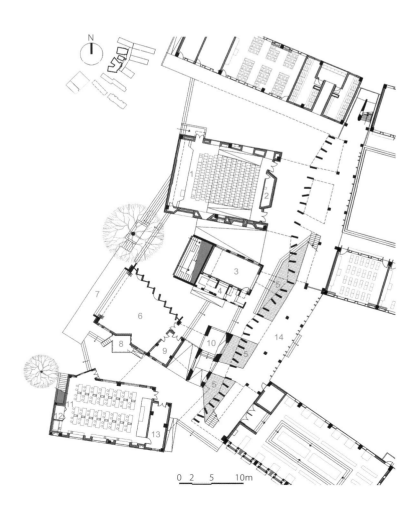

Multi-Functional Classrooms
Ground Floor (Right):
1. Auditorium
2. Projection room
3. Group activity room
4. Play space
5. Pool
6. Music classroom
7. Stage
8. Slide
9. Musical instruments room
10. Vestibule
11. Laboratory
12. Storage
13. Preparation room
14. Linking corridor (spine)

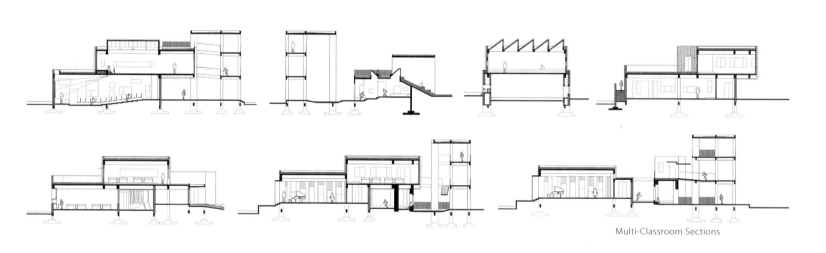

Multi-Classroom Sections

8, 9. Passage space

connecting to the existing kitchen to form an integrated whole. With the sloping roof, the courtyard feels friendly and comfortable, with spaces of various scales. The bamboo suspended ceiling further enhanced the cosy feel. The openings on the walls are well proportioned for children, solving the problems of view, ventilation and sun shade on different heights.

Construction

Different from conventional cases of transporting workers, materials and techniques from other areas, the project aims to realise localisation in the construction process. Its core lies in consideration for local climate, use of local materials and crafts, and applying building techniques suitable for the local case.

To be specific, the architects used local materials such as shale black bricks, timber and bamboo. After the earthquake, the town was short of bricks, and the bricks used came from different brickkilns near Deyang. The different bricks were used for different buildings, and thanks to their

9

scattered positions and different scales, they wouldn't seem awkward and were completed in stages. Timber processing has a long history in Xiaoquan Town, and wood is plenty for use. In the project, timber is extensively used in door and window. Fixed glass windows and flexible wooden windows make the elevations tidy and clear. Local bamboos are used on the façades and suspended ceilings, acting as heat insulation and enriching the visual experience. Besides, recycled bricks are used in outdoor paving and benches, symbolically giving them a rebirth in reconstruction.

Concrete structure cast in site is applied in the reconstruction. The beams, columns and concrete walls are exposed with no decoration. The composite walls are wrapped with bricks and filled with thermal insulation materials. All these elements are clearly shown on the facades. The dormitory building uses bricks and concrete as load-bearing structure to reduce cost. The exterior is wrapped with black bricks, with structural columns, window lintels and floor slabs seen outside, so the structure of the building is obvious.

The project was initiated in December 2008; construction started in April 2009 and completed in September 2010. The Deyang-based contractor, Huaxiluyi Construction Co., Ltd., was dutiful in the construction and guaranteed the architectural quality. Particularly for the concrete cast in site, with few experience they made experiments on site to find effective technical solutions. However, concrete construction is always liable to make some mistakes on site. For example, slightly different casting time control leads to uneven wall surfaces, which are polished later. Therefore, some surfaces are left with such special textures and are preserved to show the true characteristics of current constructing techniques and to enrich the material. The final cost of the project is lower than 1,500RMB per square metre, achieving a successful budget management. The reconstructed Ethnic Elementary School has been put into use since October 2010.

10

10. Courtyard
11. Linking space
12. Terrace between big steps and linking space
13, 14. Linking space

Ground Floor Plan:
1. Sports apparatus room
2. Computer facilities
3. Computer room
4. Toilet
5. Teacher duty room
6. Classroom
7. Auditorium
8. Group activity room
9. Play space
10. Music classroom
11. Music instruments room
12. Slide
13. Vestibule
14. Laboratory
15. Preparation room
16. Reading room
17. Dormitory
18. Duty room
19. Linking corridor (spine)

Here are some descriptions of the new school from the pupils:

Entering the school, I immediately saw several buildings well arranged. I felt I was in a maze, going here and there just like an ant on a hot pan, and couldn't find my way. I was so exited at the thought of studying here and scampered around the school.

LI Xin, Class Five Grade Six

The windows were redesigned as comfortable wooden shelters protecting us from sunshine. There are steps beside the reading room where we can sit down reading interesting books at ease.

LI Zhuman, Class One Grade Five

Another interesting place in our school is the so-called "bomb shelter", which is constituted by several concrete stages. After class we play games or read books there. There are several openings for look-out, through which we can see the Music Hall while playing games. A staircase is located in the middle of the corridor, connecting the classrooms and playground. Here high and low steps are well proportioned and arranged: on the low steps we can scamper like rabbits, while on the high steps we can sit down to read a book.

CHEN Jiayu, Class Two Grade Five

The new school is a beautiful mini-city. I think there should be a library in our school, where we can know more about the fantastic world.

CAI Siqi, Class One Grade Four

Standing in front of the teaching building, you must be feeling puzzled and thinking "Which way should I take?" That's it! The teaching building is like a maze where you have to ponder the way every step you take.

WAN Yao, Class Six Grade Six

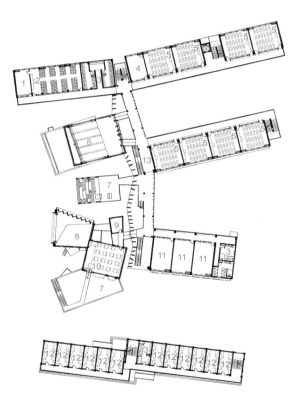

First Floor Plan:
1. Computer facilities
2. Computer room
3. Toilet
4. Teacher duty room
5. Classroom
6. Art classroom
7. Roof terrace
8. Void
9. Preparation room
10. Laboratory
11. Office
12. Dormitory
13. Linking corridor (spine)

12. Terrace between big steps and linking space
13, 14. Linking space

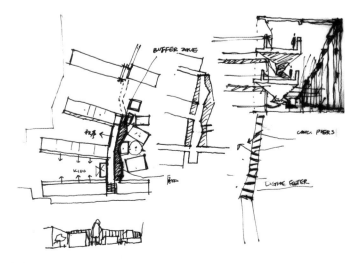

15

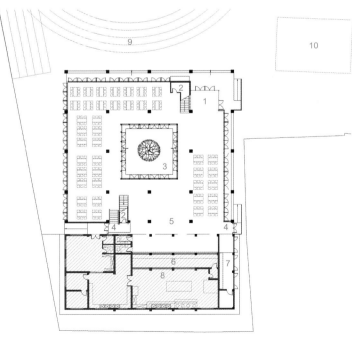

Ground Floor Plan of Dining Hall:
1. Main entrance
2. Storage
3. Patio
4. Secondary entrance
5. Queue area
6. Food window
7. Dishwashing
8. Existing kitchen
9. Sports court
10. Dormitory

15. First floor of dining hall
16. Façade of dining hall
17. Openings on multi-purpose classrooms wall
18. Interior of multi-purpose classroom

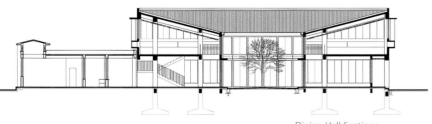

Dining Hall Sections

199

17. Openings on multi-purpose classrooms wall
18. Interior of multi-purpose classroom

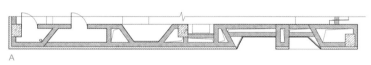

A

B

C

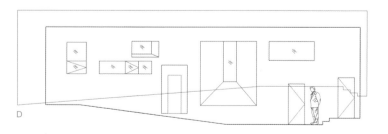

D

Wall Detail:
A. Enlarged plan, South wall, Auditorium (level 0.9m)
B. Enlarged plan, South wall, Auditorium (level 1.8m)
C. Enlarged plan, South wall, Auditorium (level 2.6m)
D. Elevation, South wall, Auditorium

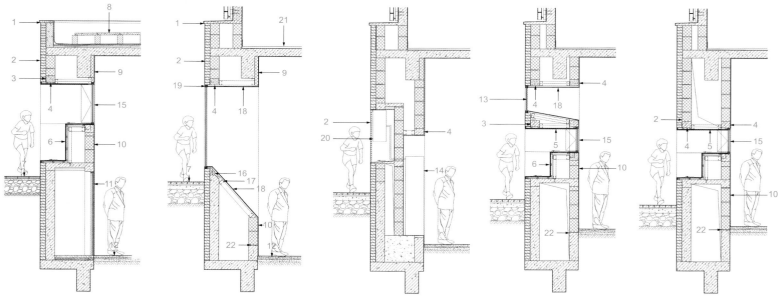

Wall Detail, South Wall, Auditorium (Above):
1. Concrete coping
2. 120mm brick
   200mm aerated concrete block
   15mm gypsum plastering
3. 115/115mm steel angle
4. Concrete lintel
5. Wooden board
6. Wooden chair
   20mm timber board
   Wood batten
   Waterproof layer

Plywood
Steel stud
7. 240/115/53mm brick
   30mm screed
   300mm sandstone
   Tamped soil
8. 495/495/50mm precast concrete pane
   115/115/200mm brick support
   4mm waterproof layer
   20mm screed
   50mm polystyrene thermal insulation
   Reinforced concrete roof

9. Thermal insulation block
10. White paint
    8mm screed
    200mm aerated concrete block
11. White paint wooden door
12. 40mm fine aggregate concrete
    1.5mm waterproof layer
    30mm screed
    60mm concrete
    Tamped soil
13. Double glazing fixed window
14. A.C unit

15. Openable window
16. Wooden batten
17. Steel frame
18. White paint
    8mm screed
    15mm gypsum board
    Steel frame
19. 50x50mm steel angle window frame
20. Grey aluminium alloy shutter
21. 40mm fine aggregate concrete
    Reinforced concrete slab
22. 20 mm cement screed dampproof

MAOPING VILLAGE SCHOOL
Leiyang City, Hunan Province
in+of architecture, Studio Wang Lu of Tsinghua University

Site Area: 5,273m²
Gross Floor Area: 1,168m²
Design/Completion Time: 2006/2008
Architect: in+of architecture, Studio Wang Lu of Tsinghua University
Design Team: WANG Lu, LU Jiangsong, HUAN Huaihai, ZHENG Xiaodong
Collaborator: School of Architecture, Hunan University
Sponsor/Client: Zhejiang Association of Commerce in Hunan Province
Contractor: Farmers from Maoping Village
Photographer: Christians Richter, WANG Lu
Awards: Chicago International Architecture Awards, 2010;
Architectural Design Merit Award, Architectural Society of China, 2008

On July 19, 2006, rainstorms and mountain floods caused by Typhoon "Bilis" destroyed the buildings of the primary school in Maoping Village. Zhejiang Association of Commerce in Hunan Province urgently raised 500,000 RMB on July 29, 2006 for building a new primary school – Maoping Village School. The money was used for ground-levelling, playground facilities, desks and blackboards, school uniforms, and so on. The total floor area of the school is 1,168 square metres, and the actual construction cost (including interior plaster rendering) is 300,000 RMB, which amounts to 300 RMB per square metre.

Voluntarily undertaking the task of designing the Maoping Village School, Studio Wang Lu started site analysis on August 5, 2006. Together with local villagers, they completed the construction of the new primary school on December 8, 2007. The whole process lasted for sixteen months.

Leiyang, located in the south of Hunan Province, is the home place of Cai Lun, the inventor of paper-making in the Eastern Han Dynasty. Maoping, which is 30 kilometres to the south of Leiyang, is a small mountain village with its simple folkways. Surrounded by hills on all sides, the village and its houses continuously spread out by following the topographical contours of hills and valleys, with the ancestral shrine at its centre. Along with the development of economy and the advancement of urbanisation, great changes are taking place in Maoping Village, as in the vast rural areas of China.

The site of the primary school is on the slope in the northeast of Maoping Village. The two-storey school building stands on a terraced ground that is embedded in the slope. The configuration, cross-section, materials and colours of the building are basically isomorphic to local houses, and the scale of its gables is largely commensurate with the surrounding houses. The division of the structure by small sky-wells that correspond to teachers'

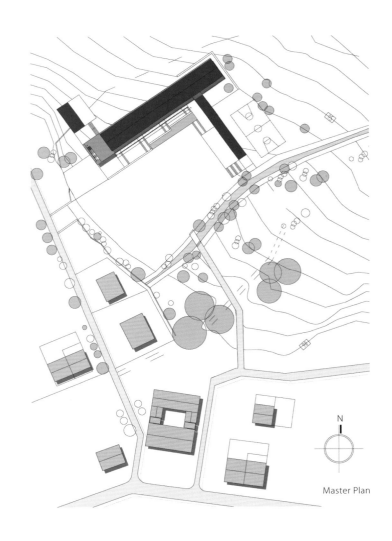

Master Plan

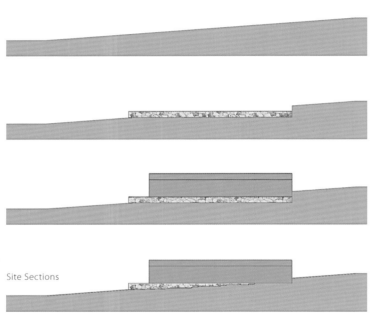

Site Sections

offices and staircases renders the whole building resembling a cluster of local houses; through the breaking-up of the whole, the school amicably blends with the local environment. In order to keep the construction cost under control and to adapt the project to local construction techniques, bricks are employed as the main building material: red bricks are used for the building so as to have a better dialogue with the surrounding houses, whereas the limited amount of large grey bricks are applied to roads, paths, and open grounds.

The design began with learning local residents' way of life and interpreting local residential buildings. Containing solutions for local design problems, local experience of building formed a basis for the exploration of new architectural expressions. With a modernist sensibility, the architects sought to invoke the essential spirit of local culture, and at the same time relate it with contemporary life. In this way, not only is the new primary school endowed with memory of the past, keeping alive the good tradition of local residential buildings in their appropriate adaptation to the local conditions, but, while revealing local characteristics, it can also open-heartedly constitute a place with a spirit of times and a real sense of culture, so as to expand the values of local culture, and represent the humanistic character of the particular building type as embodied in the school.

The northern brick façade has a few brick lattice works piercing through each of the wall, a measure of architectural treatment that was derived from the tradition of local houses, where this technique had been applied in order to reduce deadweight of the wall and to ensure ventilation. The largest wall with lattice work of this kind on the north side of the lobby becomes the only "decoration" for the lobby space, and entering the lobby, one is presented with a digitalised scene of the outside landscape, making the space distinctive.

The southern façade, with wooden framework screen as its integral part, similarly borrowed the language of local architecture, so that the building was instilled with certain symbolic significance. Like an unfolded role of bamboo slips for writing in ancient China, the façade gains an air of scholarship for the primary school building. The corridor on the first floor is thereby distinctive: when one looks out into distance, it seems as if the landscape is present behind a stretch of woods, and the building therefore is not only an architectural structure but also a toy with intersected light and shadow, which children can enter, and with which remain the special memories of living in Maoping.

1. Terrace at the main entrance
2. Southeast view
3. Steps at the entrance
4. South façade
5. Landscape view

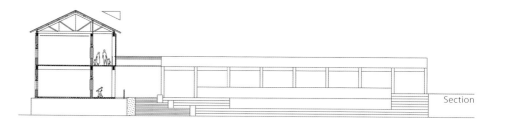

Section

6

Maoping Village School was built at a low-cost as a site-adaptive rural primary school, to which local building materials were applied, and in the construction of which local residents participated. It not only features the local character and humanistic connotations, but also is enriched with the spirit of the times. The practice of its design was one of the Studio's explorations of building in economically disadvantaged areas, and of making creative efforts in the process of cultural and technical continuation. The process of building a learning place for children itself is also a rare educational experience.

6. North façade
7. West brick wall
8. Stairs in the hallway

North Bird's-eye View

8

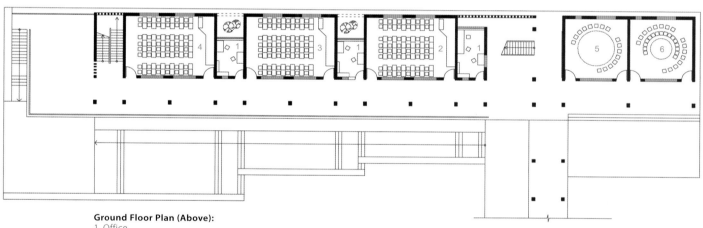

Ground Floor Plan (Above):
1. Office
2. Classroom for grade 1
3. Classroom for grade 2
4. Classroom for grade 3
5. Activity room
6. Children's room

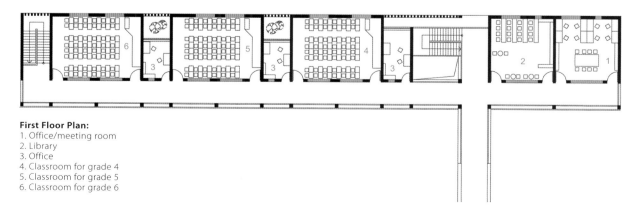

First Floor Plan:
1. Office/meeting room
2. Library
3. Office
4. Classroom for grade 4
5. Classroom for grade 5
6. Classroom for grade 6

9

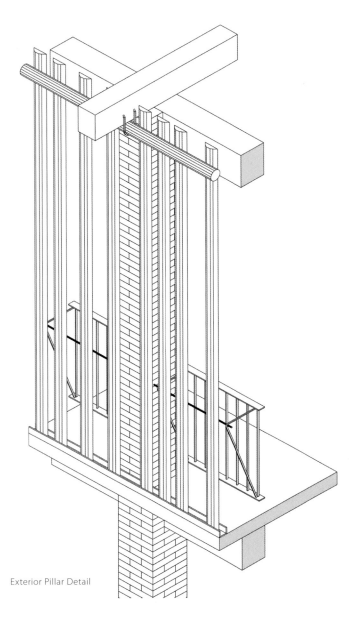

Exterior Pillar Detail

10

9. Ground floor corridor
10. Classroom
11. First floor corridor
12. Façade concept

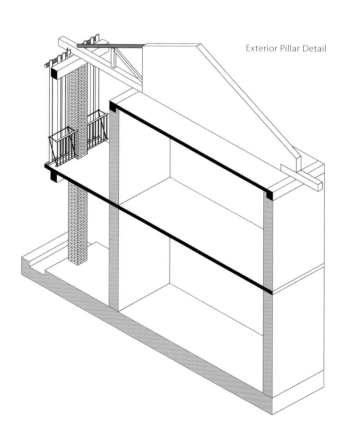

Exterior Pillar Detail

11

12

PRIMARY SCHOOL AT HEIHU VILLAGE
Mao County, Sichuan Province
BCKJ Architects

Site Area: 6,482.4m²
Gross Floor Area: 4,409.04m²
Completion Time: 2010
Architect: BCKJ Architects
Design Team: DONG Mei, LIU Xiaochuan, ZHANG Yang, YAN Haisong, SHAO Wenwei, XU Gang
Structure Architect: Institute of Residential Building Design & Research Co., Ltd., Beijing
Photographer: LIU Xiaochuan, DONG Mei

Background

After the 5.12 Wenchuan Earthquake in 2008, the Primary School at Heihu Village in Mao County, Sichuan was built. The project was sponsored by One Foundation from Shanghai and was organised by an association from Beijing called Friend of Nature. The boarding school opened on October 2010. From design conception to material selection to construction, the project was dedicated to green concepts such as environmentally-friendly architecture, energy saving and resource recycling, and resulted in a sustainable new school, which is now the place for Friend of Nature to give lectures on environmental protection. In this way, green concepts are carried forward from architecture to education.

The primary school was located on the east of the township government building, 27 kilometres from the town. The boarding school accommodates eight classes, with 320 pupils and 24 teachers. The building complex includes five sections: 1. teaching building (with offices); 2. canteen for students; 3. dormitory for students; 4. dormitory for teachers; 5. outdoor facilities.

Design Concepts and Features

1. Green Architecture Concepts: Basic Technology, Low Cost, Low Carbon, and Zero Emission
1). Local material and architectural language
a. Rubble stone is readily available in the village and extensively used in the construction. Therefore, cost on material transportation was effectively reduced. And, local traditional wall construction technique is properly adopted.
b. The walls are constructed with a thermal insulation layer made of rigid polyurethane foam and cement gel with rice hulls. The walls are more solid and meanwhile, cheap local materials – rice hull, for example – help enhance their thermal performance.

Site Plan (Below):
1. Teaching building
2. Office building and multi-functional hall
3. Students' dormitory
4. Teachers' dormitory
5. Dining hall, kitchen and hot water room
A. Eco-poll: tertiary treatment of waste water, which is then discharged into river
B. Mini eco-wetland: secondary treatment of waste water
C. Septic tank: sanitary sewage treatment and providing partial fuel for kitchen
D. Solar photovoltaic panels: providing school living water
E. Mini eco-wetland: primary treatment of sanitary waste water
F. Mini eco-wetland: primary treatment of sanitary waste water

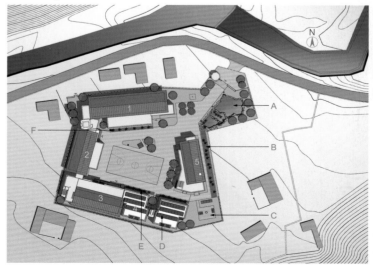

1. Surrounding topography
2. School context
3. Bird's-eye view

South Elevation

West Elevation

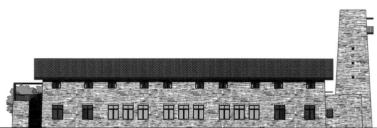
North Elevation

East Elevation

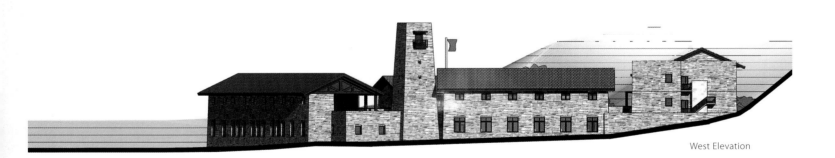
West Elevation

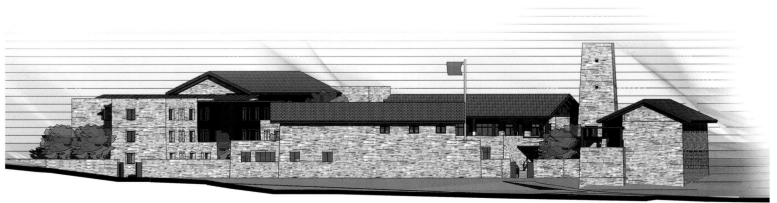
East Elevation

4. Basketball court
5. Distant view of Teaching Building

c. Locally processed double-layer glass windows with wooden frames are adopted to reduce thermal lost.

2). Energy saving
a. A solar energy collector system is installed on the roof of teachers' dormitory. It provides hot water for students' bath and the kitchen.
b. Solar photoelectric technology is adopted to supply lighting power.
c. Since local water and electricity are not expensive, the architects reserved places and outlets for future electric radiators, and outlets for future induction cookers in the kitchen.
d. The energy consumption of the school is estimated as 30kwh/year.

3). Waste dumping and reuse
a. Bricks and stone of the earthquake-demolished buildings are used for back filling of the site.
b. Methane septic tanks are built to supply fuels for the kitchen, and liquid methane and organic manure for nearby farmers.
c. Urine is collected to provide highly-efficient organic manure for nearby farmers.
d. Garbage sorting. Garbage from kitchen, fallen leaves, and other organics are collected in the tanks as raw materials. Students participate in the garbage sorting to experience natural recycling.
e. Three small wetlands are built to process sanitary waste. Water from hand washing, bath and kitchen (after oil-separation process) is discharged into the wetlands. In this way, the environment is protected and a special landscape in the school is created.
f. An eco-pool is built for students to study the water quality and water plants, and also for further purification of grey water. Students take part in the planting and maintenance to witness the purification process.
g. Exhaust from the kitchen is processed before emitting into the air, reducing pollution as much as possible.

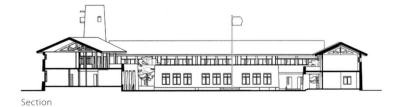

Section

h. Rain water is collected on the roofs for courtyard sweeping and plants irrigation. Students participate in the process to experience water recycling.
i. Water-permeable bricks are used for courtyard paving, protecting underground water resources.

4). Energy-saving equipments
a. Energy-saving and fluorescent lamps are adopted instead of incandescent ones.
b. Water-saving sanitary equipments such as taps are used.
c. Solar lamps are used for courtyard lighting.

5). Social sustainability
a. Traditional building materials (such as rubble stone) and local construction techniques are adopted.
b. It is an open school in which the library is open to villagers and the multi-purpose hall can be used for villager training.
c. The solid school architecture becomes an emergency shelter.
d. It is a low-cost, green school. With a total cost of 9,785,000RMB (2,219RMB/m²), the project successfully balanced the budget. Almost all the cost was used on improvement of safety and other properties of the building. Students' chairs are all old ones. Building material prices were unexpectedly high due to the earthquake and the traffic problem it caused, so the actual cost is 16% higher than the budget. The solar photoelectric panels are donated by the factory.
With green concepts, the project achieved the eco-friendly goals of "basic technology, low cost, low carbon and zero emission". The school is where environmental protection awareness starts for the students. With traditional architectural language, the school is perfectly integrated into the local context. For the local people, the project is a successful case of carrying out sustainable concepts in their hometown reconstruction, complying with national rules on construction.

With safe and friendly buildings, green and lively playground, the school is a harmonious element in the village and acts as a place of communication between the town and village. It is a Qiang ethnic minority village, and dignity and pride of the ethnicity are integrated into the school, which is endowed with heart and soul and thus becomes a school with emotion, responsibility and hope, a school to leave you beautiful memories. The primary school is expected to be an exemplary project about how to harmonise architecture with local contexts.

2. Design Features
1. The school architecture is decomposed into sections with residential scales, which are interrelated and integrated into the village. The building and spaces are designed to suit local climate and regional characteristics.

2. The village in which the school is located is a traditional Qiang ethnic village. The neighbouring Heihu Qiang Camp on the hillside is a famous cultural heritage. The school buildings used traditional architectural language of local residences, simplified and developed it with contemporary construction techniques. The architects paid homage to the local culture and hoped the school to be inspiring for future projects.

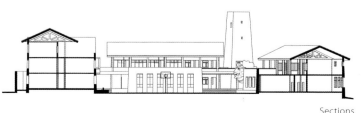

Sections

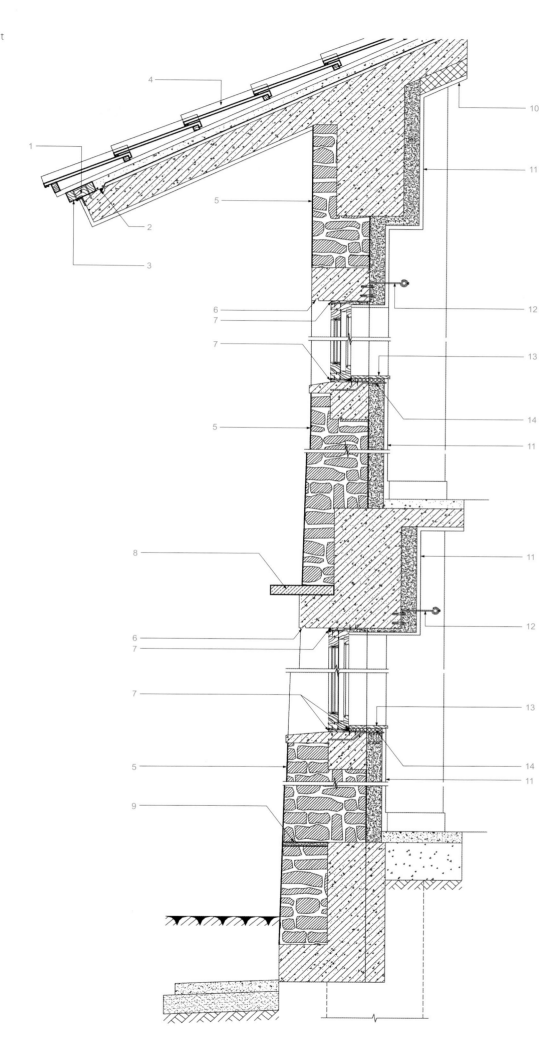

6. View of Teaching Building from basketball court
7. Rain water collection with simple equipment
8. Campus

Façade Detail (Right):
1. 150×50 wood border
2. Seal
3. L50×50×7-50
   @500
4. Roof 2
5. Façade 1
6. 15×10 water drop
7. Seal
8. Rubble stone cornice
   (same width as beam)
9. 20mm waterproof mortar
10. Ceiling
11. Interior wall 1
12. Curtain pole
13. 15mm wood windowsill
14. 20mm polyphenyl filler

9. Space in front of Teaching Building
10. Exterior main staircase

3. The contradiction between the utilisation of local material (rubble stone) and the requirement for 8-grade anti-earthquake structure is solved. With built-in columns and scattered concrete reinforcing grids, the otherwise loose structure became solid and compact. With the idea of "rebirth after the disaster", the school is an emergency shelter for the village as well.

4. The design contains careful consideration and convenience for the students. For the master plan, direction of the sunshine and wind in the mountainous region is well considered to make the school be bathed in warm natural light. For circulation, sheltered galleries are designed between different programme sections. Due to the limited site area, the architects made use of the roof to create a terrace for communication and activity for students on the first floor in class intervals. In village schools, dry latrines are built in school corners conventionally, but here water toilets are conveniently set in both teaching and living sections. On the ground floor, barrier-free facilities are adopted; for example, ramps are set to replace steps, and other barrier-free facilities in washrooms and bathrooms. The wavy washbasin is a considerate design for students with different heights.

10

11

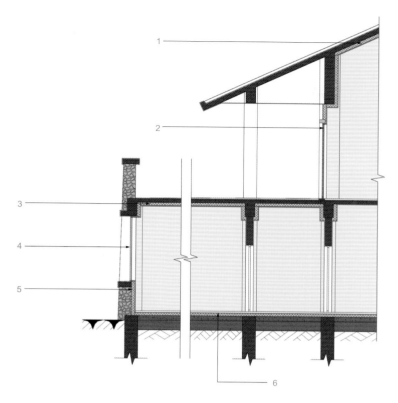

Use of Cheap Local Materials:
1. Roof thermal insulation, 100mm rice husk ash
2. Door and window thermal insulation, wooden door
3. Roof thermal insulation, 100mm rice husk ash
4. Door and window thermal insulation, double glazing window
5. Wall thermal insulation, 100mm rice husk ash
6. Floor thermal insulation, 100mm rigid polyurethane foams

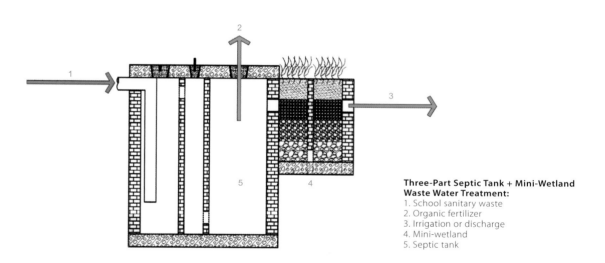

Three-Part Septic Tank + Mini-Wetland Waste Water Treatment:
1. School sanitary waste
2. Organic fertilizer
3. Irrigation or discharge
4. Mini-wetland
5. Septic tank

Methane Tank - Providing Fuel for School Kitchen and Promoting Eco-Agriculture:
1. Human excrement
2. Cattle excrement
3. Straw
4. Other organism
5. Eco-agriculture
6. Cultivation
7. Septic tank
8. Outlet
9. Methane fuel
10. Residents in the neighbourhood
11. School kitchen
12. Input

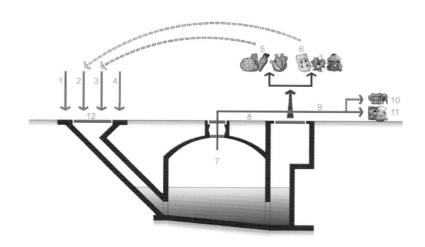

12. Teaching Building close-up view
13. Space for activities at break time
14. Veranda with columns wrapped by straw ropes

Straw Rope Detail:
1. Φ6 bolt
   @150
2. L40×25×3
   Rope end pined
   around column
3. L40×25×3
   Rope end pined
   around column
4. Φ6 bolt
   @150
5. Φ20 rope
6. Seal
7. Roof 1

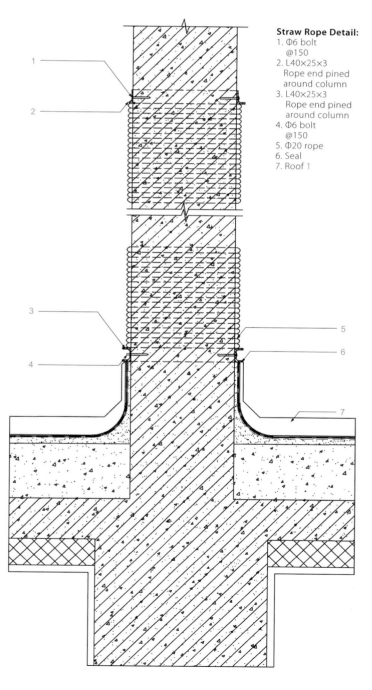

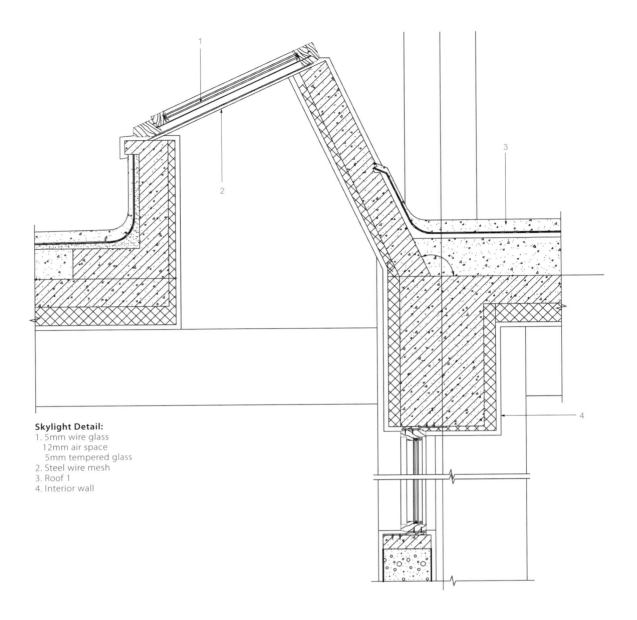

Skylight Detail:
1. 5mm wire glass
   12mm air space
   5mm tempered glass
2. Steel wire mesh
3. Roof 1
4. Interior wall

15. Classroom interior

First floor plan (Below):
1. Classroom
2. Activity terrace
3. Science activity room
4. Teaching office
5. Meeting room
   /teachers' library
6. Political affairs office
7. Washroom
8. Students dormitory
9. Teachers dormitory
10. Dining hall
11. Roof terrace

Second Floor Plan (Below):
1. Students dormitory
2. Teachers dormitory
3. Roof terrace
4. Washroom
5. Female toilet
6. Male toilet

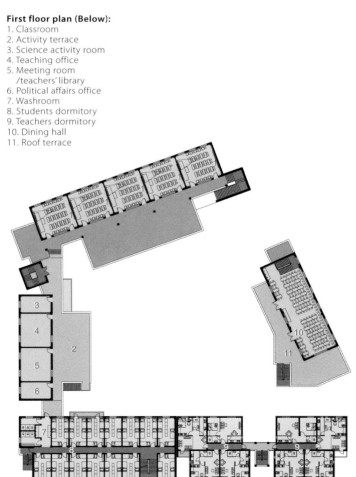

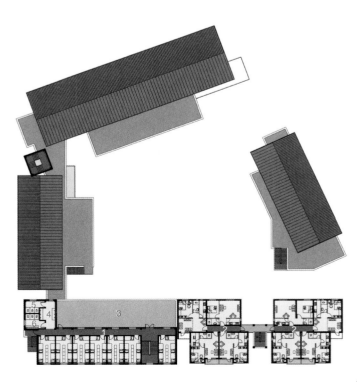

225

ECO PRIMARY SCHOOL AT MAOSI VILLAGE
Qingyang City, Gansu Province
WU Enrong, MU Jun

Gross Floor Area: 1,006m²
Design/Completion Time: 2004-2006/2007
Architect: WU Enrong/School of Architecture, The Chinese University of Hong Kong (CUHK); MU Jun/ School of Architecture, Xi'an University of Architecture and Technology
Photographer: MU Jun
Client: Education Bureau of Xifeng District
Cost: 728,000 RMB (515 RMB/m² for classrooms)

The famous Loess Plateau in northwest China is one of the poorest regions in the vast country, where local people face great challenges in developing eco architecture because of the backward in economy and technology. The Eco Primary School at Maosi Village completed in the summer of 2007 is an exemplary project under such circumstances. With the help from the local government, the architects, apart from designing, were also in charge of collecting donations and organising construction in the charity programme. The goal is not only to create a comfortable learning environment for the children, but also more importantly to develop a practical eco-architecture system suitable for local conditions.

This project features systematic and duplicatable design approaches, including three basic stages: analysing existing facts, experimenting with models, and designing and constructing. First of all, after fully studying local conditions such as cold winter and warm summer, limited budget and architectural resource, the traditional raw-soil building type in the locale, the architects decided to adopt the eco-friendly thermal design method to reduce the building's energy consumption and pollution in the cold winter. Meanwhile, they were greatly inspired by the local natural raw-soil architecture (cave dwelling). The conception and construction of the school should basically abide by four principles: comfortable interiors, minimum energy consumption and pollution, low cost, and easy construction. Based on these principles, the architects used the classrooms as a model, on which they applied the TAS software to make thermal experiments. They selected from – and sometimes optimised – local regular and natural materials, traditional building techniques and eco-design systems, and found that the very basic building technique – heat accumulator and heat insulator with raw soil and other natural materials – is the most economic and effective solution to improve architectural thermal performance and to reduce energy consumption and pollution. Therefore, this building technique is applied to the design of the classrooms.

According to the site, the ten classrooms are composed of five units located on two terraces with different levels, each classroom being able to have maximum natural light and ventilation in summer. The courtyard with ample greenery helps create an enjoyable environment for the children. The form of the classrooms is derived from the local traditional wooden-structure residence with pitched roofs. Hence, the anti-seismic property of wooden structures is preserved, while construction is comparatively easy for the villagers. The classrooms on the north are embedded into the terrace. In this way, sufficient daylight from the south is guarantied while heat loss in winter is effectively minimised. Thick adobe walls, traditional roofs with insulation layers, double-glazing… These heat accumulators and heat insulators are helpful to withstand the harsh weather and maintain the interiors warm and cosy. In addition, some openings are specially adjusted to maximally bring in natural light.

The construction of the school is done in accordance with local conventions – all the builders are Maosi villagers and all the construction work is completed with common farm tools, except for excvavtors used in rough grading. Besides, most of the materials are locally obtained, such as adobe, thatch and reed. Because these raw materials are renewable, all the leftover bits and pieces could be re-used immediately after simple processing. For example, the adobe is made from the loess excavated from the ground; adobe pieces could be mixed with ryegrass as a kind of cement; the leftover pieces of wood could be used in walls and other facilities in the school. In this way, the architects appropriately exercised local architectural wisdom, successfully reducing energy consumption and pollution caused by the construction.

1. A glimpse of the basketball playground
2. School buildings
3. Bird's-eye view

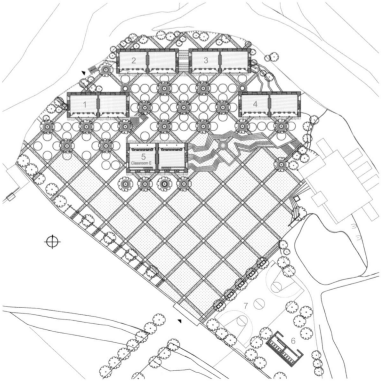

Site Plan (Left):
1. Classroom A
2. Classroom B
3. Classroom C
4. Classroom D
5. Classroom E
6. Eco-toilet
7. Basketball court

4

The new classrooms are very low-cost, with only 515 RMB per square metre, surprisingly lower than local schools built with clay bricks and concrete. The classrooms have been put in use for a year, and they are proved to have a better thermal performance than other local schools. The classrooms remained warm and fresh without burning any fuel in the rarely cold winter.

From the effect in use, the architects concluded three points. Firstly, the new school is a comfortable and pleasing learning environment for children. The architecture surpasses local buildings in terms of thermal property, energy saving and environmental protection. Secondly, many villagers are employed in the construction, who benefited from the charity project. Lastly, and more importantly, they got a chance to know more about their tradition. The primary school points out a new way to develop eco-friendly architecture in the Loess Plateau region. As proved, with a limited budget, the villagers could use their familiar traditional techniques and locally available natural materials to improve their living conditions and at the same time maximally reduce environmental pollution, eventually realising a harmonious relationship between human, architecture and nature. The project report has been written up, ready for publication and propaganda

in the future, but the architects' work has not finished. They will further their research in eco-friendly architecture, not only for the primary school, but more importantly for the future architecture in the region.

"From now on, we don't need to burn coal for heating in our school. The money saved could be used to buy children more books," said The headmaster of Eco Primary School at Maosi Village.

4. Front view
5. Reed laying of the roof
6. Steps at the square
7. Square overview
8. Square view

5

6

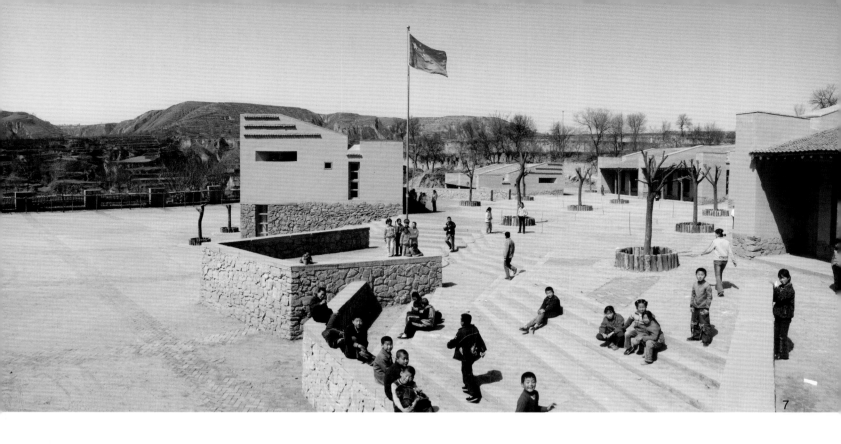

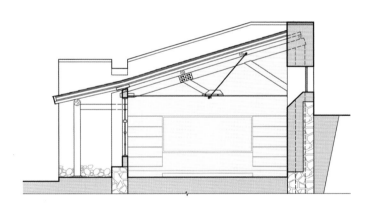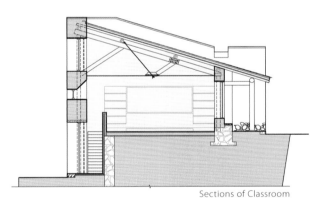

Sections of Classroom

9. West view
10. Exterior view of the classroom
11. South veranda
12, 13. Classroom interior

14, 15. Eco-toilet
16. Windows of the classroom
17. New personal space for children

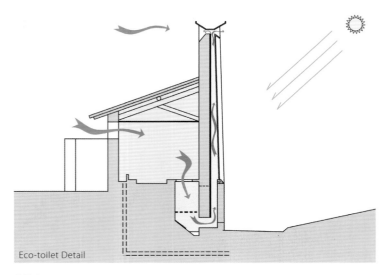

Eco-toilet Detail

BRIDGE SCHOOL
Pinghe County, Fujian Province
LI Xiaodong / Li Xiaodong Studio

Site Area: 1,550m²
Gross Floor Area: 240m²
Construction Period: 2008-2009
Architect: LI Xiaodong
Design Team: CHEN Jiansheng, LI Ye, WANG Chuan,
LIANG Qiong, LIU Mengjia, NIE Junqi
Collaborator: Hedao Architecture Design, Xiamen, Fujian
Main Materials: Steel (structure),
wood (interior & grid), concrete (base)
Client: Xiashi Village
Awards: AR Emerging Architecture Awards Winner, 2009

The Bridge, the School, the Playground and the Stage
Located at a remote village, Fujian Province, China, the project not only
provides a physical function – a school + a bridge, but also presents a
spiritual centre. There's a local legend saying that the two castles in the
village used to be enemies and thus built a creek in between. The Bridge
School connects the two castles across the river. The main concept of
the design is to enliven an old community (the village) and to sustain
a traditional culture (the castles and lifestyle) through a contemporary
language which does not compete with the traditional, but presents and
communicates with the traditional with respect. It is done by combining
a few different functions into one space – a bridge which connects two
old castles cross the creek, a school which also symbolically connects
past, current with future, a playground (for the kids) and the stage (for the
villagers).

A lightweight structure traverses a small creek in a single, supple bound.
Essentially, it is an intelligent contemporary take on the archetype of the
inhabited bridge. Supported on concrete piers (which also has the function
of a small shop), the simple steel structure acts like a giant box girder that'
s been slightly dislocated, so the building subtly twists, rises and falls as it
spans the creek. The colour of earth yellow is perfectly integrated with that
of the castles, whose circular shape sharply contrasts with the rectangular
structure, creating continuity and harmony.

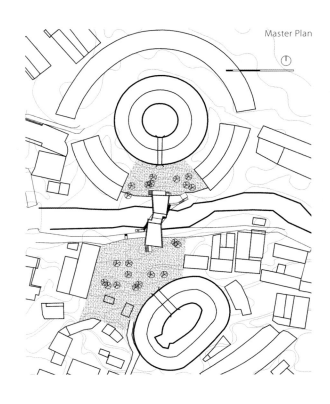

Master Plan

The unique archetype of castle reveals the culture the ethnic group, especially their past of defensive living and homeless life. Such a culture has cumulated rich legacy and unique appeal for the village. Meanwhile, it also caused the close-castle lifestyle for each family, refusing outsiders. In between the castles there are usually mud lands, hard to stand on, which lead to the lack of public space for communication. A primary school perhaps would bring some changes to the primordial spatial system. The particular site of the building gave the architect the initial idea – a bridge connecting the two castles across the creek.

Inside are a pair of almost identical, wedge-shaped classrooms, each tapering towards the mid point of the structure (which holds a small public library). Although it's possible to use the building as a bridge, a narrow crossing suspended underneath the steel structure and anchored by tensile wires offers an alternative and more direct route. Both ends of the building are equipped with sliding and folding doors, making the spaces outside of the classrooms become stages for the villagers. The classrooms are used as

performing platforms after class so as to makes a functional and formal link between the castles, as well as reorganising the surroundings and providing a public square for the village. On one side of the square is the circular, crude castle, while on the other side sit the well-defined stages – the contrastive dialogue between the two sides makes the space full of tension. At dusk and at night, active villagers gather here. Catalysing a sense of history, the project is more than just a school, but a social centre of the entire village.

Architecture built in a historical context is liable to suffer two extremes: one is to extensively adopt modern technologies, and the other is to highlight the primordial feel with a nostalgic atmosphere. In the Bridge School project, the architect didn't stick to local materials, and sought to find a solution between the two extremes, one that uses a modest yet contemporary architecture language. Steel structure is adopted for the building, and the entire interior is used mainly as two classrooms. For the exterior skin, wooden grid (size 10×15×20) is adopted in order to protect the interior views not to be interfered by passers-by, as well as to bring in

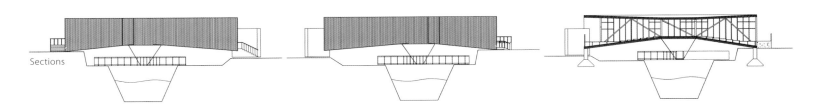

Sections

238

1. Bridge School with a box structure
2. Connection between the two castles
3. Steel bridge under the Bridge School

the beautiful creek scenery outside. Physical lightness and spatial fluidity are keys. The steel frame is wrapped in a veil of slim timber slats, which filter light and temper the interior with cooling breeze. Underneath this structure is a zigzag public bridge, which would not conflict with the two squares at both ends. The modest yet contemporary language creates a poetic space without big volume or showy details. With an assurance that belies its rustic setting, the new building also acts as a foil to the mass and weight of the neighbouring historical structures.

The castle community has old and regular spaces. On such a "Tabula Rasa" formed with a long history, the Bridge School acts as a kind of interference. The architect tries to solve the contradiction between the closed living system and modern lifestyle by setting a structure with modern architecture language amongst the old traditional buildings, hoping to enliven the village with refreshing vigour. In this sense, the Bridge School surpasses the basic function of a primary school, and further enriches spatial diversity of the village. The architect said that the essence of architectural design is the same as traditional Chinese medical science in which we adjust the body system to cure illness, instead of directly aiming at the illness itself. Comparing the Bridge School with Yuhu Primary School in Lijiang, a previous project of the architect, we could clearly see the totally different objectives and the same concern about environment. The Yuhu project became a model for local architecture, while the Bridge School mainly aims at providing structurally efficient public space for the community. Rural areas in China are currently welcoming the era of "New Villages" and buildings in the countryside are attracting more and more attention. Nevertheless, quintessentially it is rural community and lifestyle that we should really pay close attention to. Perhaps the Bridge School provides a new perspective to the building of New Villages in China.

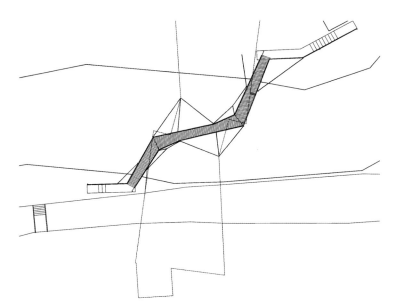

4. Panoramic view

5

6

5. Perspective
6. Slide
7. Classroom interior

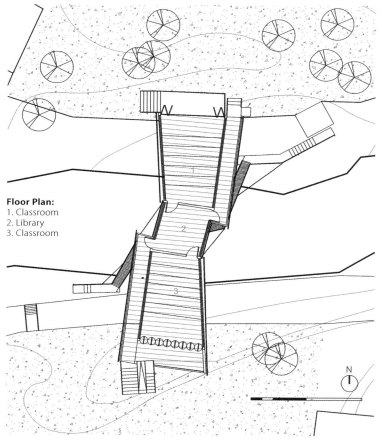

Floor Plan:
1. Classroom
2. Library
3. Classroom

NEW BUD PRIMARY SCHOOL AT XIASI VILLAGE
Guangyuan City, Sichuan Province
ZHU Jingxiang, XIA Heng /
The Chinese University of Hong Kong (CUHK)

Gross Floor Area: 437m² (Interior: 347m² ; Corridor: 180m²)
Total Volume: 1,040m³
Design/Completion Time: 2008-2009/2009
Architect: ZHU Jingxiang, XIA Heng/
The Chinese University of Hong Kong (CUHK)
Structural Engineer: KE Youlin
Capacity: 5 classrooms, 1 office, 1 toilet and 1 bathroom
System: LGS skeleton strengthened by rigid board
Comfort: A full insulated envelope + optimised daylight use + eco toilet
Sustainability: A demountable system,
paves made from recycled material
Earthquake Resistance: (Mercalli Intensity Scale) Degree X
(evaluated by Civil Engineering Department, Hong Kong University)

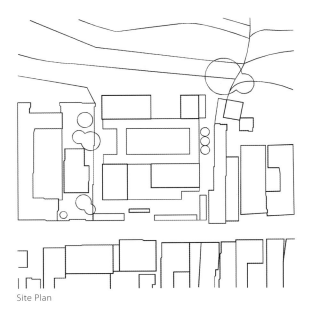
Site Plan

The tremendous loss of life and property caused by the 5.12 Wenchuan Earthquake in 2008 reveals the absence of decent structural design and adequate monitoring of the construction process in the region. Reconstruction has been difficult and a large number of temporary shelters that are neither durable nor thermally comfortable have been built in an attempt to meet the urgent needs of those affected. These shelters, when demolished later, will give rise to new construction waste.

A research team led by Prof. Zhu Jingxiang of the School of Architecture at The Chinese University of Hong Kong (CUHK) has developed an integrated light-structure system for the reconstruction of New Bud Primary School at Xiasi Village in Sichuan's Jiange County. The old building suffered serious damage in the earthquake, so its students had to walk for an hour to attend classes in another school. With the support of the Hong Kong Dragon Culture Charity Fund and the CUHK New Asia Sichuan Redevelopment Fund, the new school was completed in just two weeks and has been in operation since September. The building is safe and durable, and the cost of construction is low. It also looks attractive and features good thermal performance and a high energy-saving capacity.

The primary load-bearing part of the school is a light-gauge steel frame, which is strengthened by a prefabricated panel system. These two parts are bound together by mechanical fasteners to form a strong but light composite structure. Although the wall is only 16cm thick, the system is able to resist high seismic forces. Under the protection of the outer panel and surface coating, the life of the skeleton is expected to last over 20 years.

The school features high thermal performance, thanks to the use of thermal insulation and storage materials. It also adopts a multi-layered envelope system where the position and ratio of the doors and windows are carefully designed to ensure that classrooms will be cool in summer and warm in winter. The decentralised opening system brings in enough day-light and natural ventilation, which greatly reduces energy consumption.

Additionally, the design incorporates environmental concepts by mostly using mechanical joints instead of chemical compounds to avoid toxic emission and to facilitate maintenance and disassembly in the future. A solar water heater and an eco-friendly toilet are equipped to improve rural sanitation.

The principle of sustainability is also reflected in the choice of materials. Materials dismantled from the old school are reused as paver, spacer or thermal mass. Some of the stone bases discarded by the villagers are also reused to furnish the courtyard. Besides, no other materials except cement were purchased for construction. Old bricks, stones and tiles are reused to achieve terrazzo effects in the flooring. This encourages local workers to preserve and develop their crafts, while reducing dependence on industrialised building materials.

As all superstructure components are prefabricated in factories in Shenzhen and Chengdu, on-site assembly became an easy task. With the guidance of CUHK researchers, the 450-square-metre New Bud Primary School was built within two weeks. The new school comprises four single-storey buildings, a central courtyard, four standard classrooms, a multi-function hall, a teachers' office and an eco-friendly toilet.

Prof. Zhu said, "It takes many years for me to conceive, experiment and, finally, put such a light-structure system into practice. The success of the construction of New Bud Primary School demonstrates the significance of articulating research in design. The research brings about new ideas and methods, while the design transforms such ideas and methods into a building. This research has also ironed out the long-existing contradiction between construction speed and quality. It not only integrates the potential ability of different manufacturers, but also provides an opportunity to unite different communities and disseminate knowledge."

The building industry and the largest temporary house company on the mainland have shown great interest in the project. They have conducted site visits and explored the feasibility of technological collaboration. Mainland architects have also invited Prof. Zhu to lecture on the innovative design and the speedy construction of the school. In the final stage of construction, 30 volunteers including university students recruited from the mainland and Hong Kong, as well as architects, took part. This enabled them to experience innovative building technology and the symbiotic relationship that can exist between the rural and the urban.

1. Entrance square
2. Overview at dusk
3. Two classrooms along street

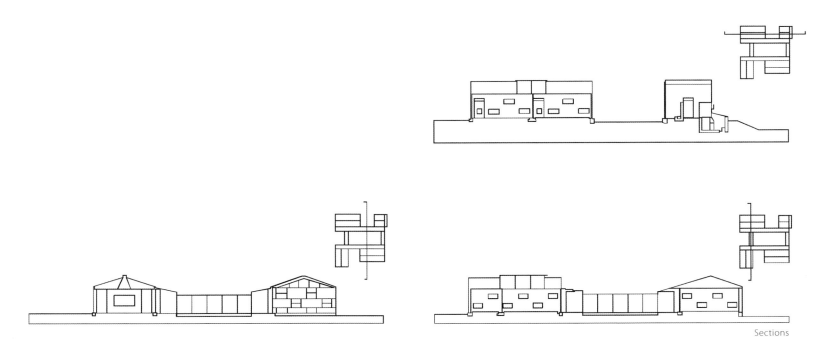

Sections

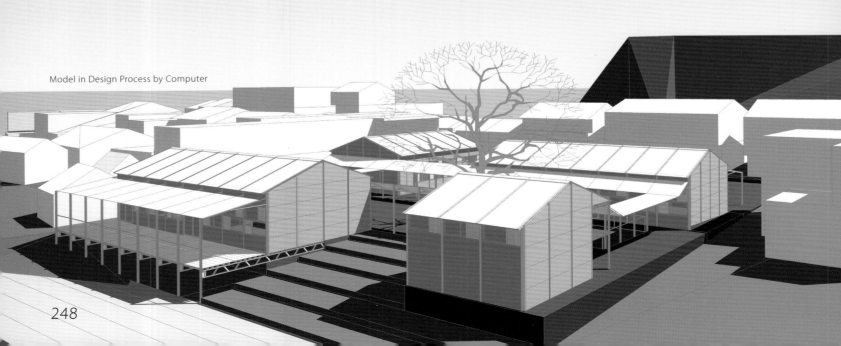

Model in Design Process by Computer

4. Bird's-eye view
5. School context

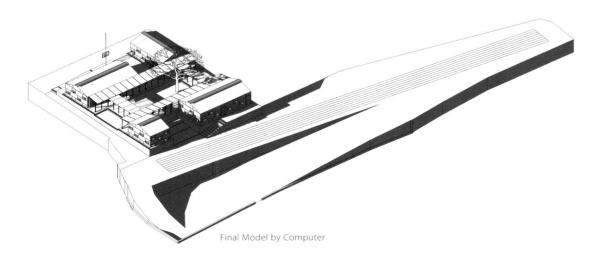

Final Model by Computer

6, 7. Construction
8. Multi-function classroom

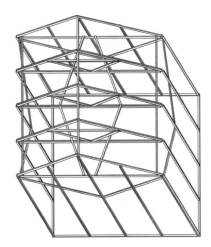

Skeleton Diagram

Skeleton Durability Diagram

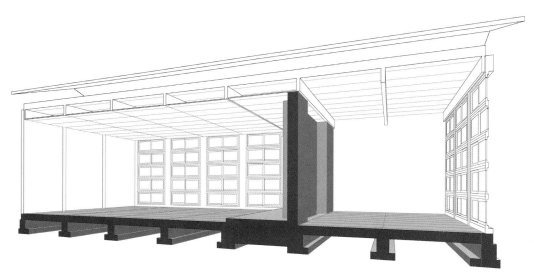

Thermal Mass for Indoor Climate Stability

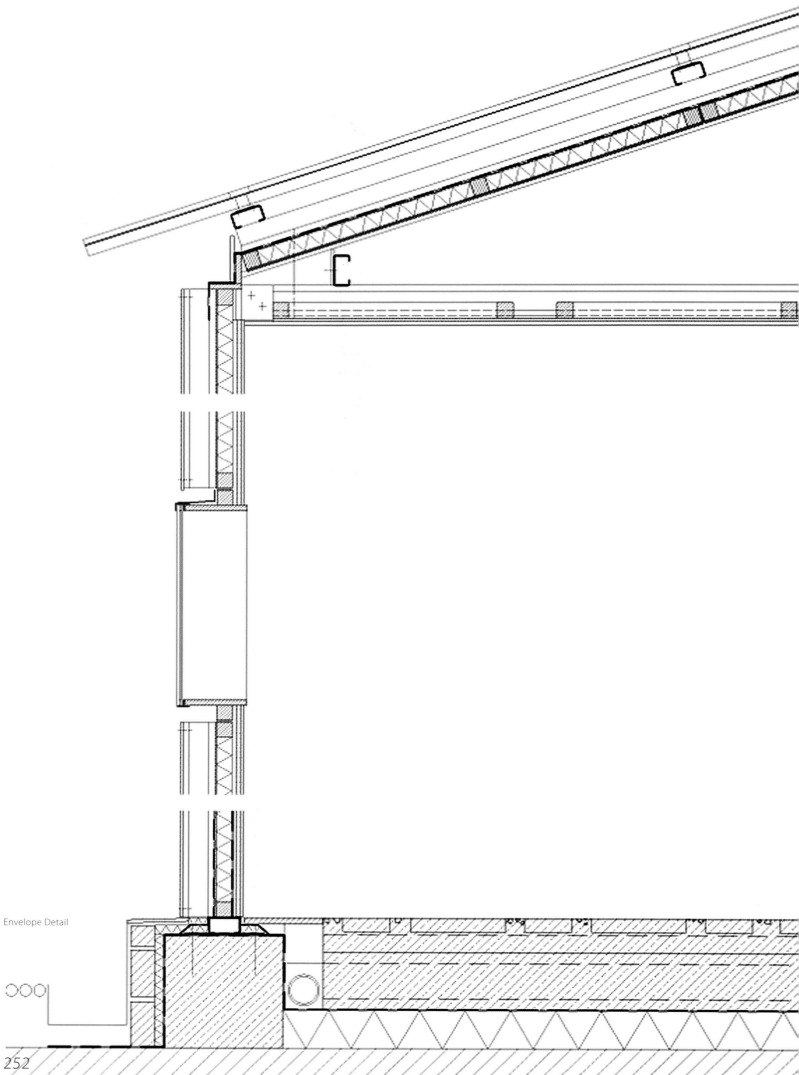

Envelope Detail

9. Classrooms along river
10. Multi-function classroom at dusk

9

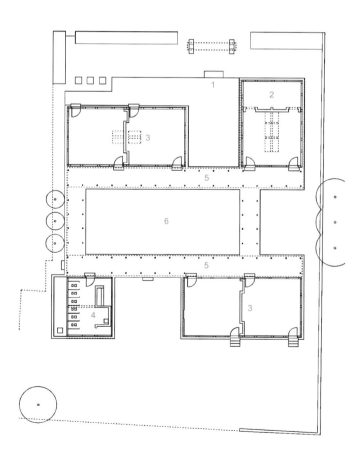

Ground Floor Plan:
1. Entrance plaza
2. Multi-functional classroom
3. Classroom
4. Eco-toilet
5. Corridor
6. Courtyard

10

ECO
World Savers

G4005

PROTECTING OUR FOOD & WATER SUPPLY

Activities To Build Awareness & Understanding

Christine Moorcroft

PROTECTING OUR FOOD AND WATER SUPPLY

Acknowledgements

Published by ECO Publishing International Ltd., 2009

ISBN 978-1-907049-04-0

The publisher can be contacted by Email at info@ecopublishinginternational.com

This resource may be used in a variety of ways; however, it is not intended that teachers or students should write into the book itself.

Every effort has been made to trace copyright holders and obtain their permission for the use of copyright material. The publisher will gladly receive information enabling them to rectify any error or omission in subsequent editions.

Photographs © Malcolm Watson, Christine Moorcroft (page 29)

Printed on recycled paper

PROTECTING OUR FOOD AND WATER SUPPLY
Contents

ECO World Savers

PROTECTING OUR FOOD AND WATER SUPPLY
Too Hot To Grow

Teacher's Guide & Planning

The Key Issues

- The Earth is becoming warmer.
- What seems like a small rise in global temperature has an enormous effect on plants.
- Crop failure is increasing.

Additional Activities

Language

- Hold a class debate on how to overcome crop failure caused by high temperatures. Different groups could prepare speeches promoting different points of view.

Science and ICT

- Plant food seeds such as cucumber, wheat, barley, tomato and raise the temperature of the area around them with heat lamps. Use a digital camera to record the changes and computer software to present them on a time-line. Compare results for the same species at different temperatures and for different species at the same temperatures at different points in their growth.

History

- Collect evidence from historical sources about effects of climate change in the past: for example, the Viking age and the 'mini Ice Age' of the sixteenth to nineteenth centuries when the Thames regularly froze over.

Geography

- Use internet sources to research the effects of global warming on crops in different countries and how this is affecting people's livelihoods.
- Find out about regions where no crops would grow if temperatures rose permanently and about those that might *benefit* from global warming, but note also the effects of flooding. Consider how the populations could survive.

Research

- Research previous periods of global warming: for example, during the tenth and eleventh centuries, when grape vines grew in the north of England and Newfoundland, and when crops flourished much farther north and at higher altitudes than at present in Scandinavia and contributed to a population rise.

More Information

Record-breaking high temperatures and drought in 2002 reduced grain harvests in India, the USA and Canada. In 2003 a late summer heat-wave in Europe reduced harvests across the continent. There was a world harvest shortfall of 94 million tons (5% of world consumption). In 2004 scientists from China, India, the Philippines and USA measured the effects of rising temperatures on rice crops: for each 1°C rise in temperature during the growing season the crop fell by 10%.

PROTECTING OUR FOOD AND WATER SUPPLY
Too Hot To Grow

The world is becoming warmer. In high temperatures leaves curl up to help keep in moisture. Plants produce food in their leaves by photosynthesis: using carbon dioxide and water to convert light energy into sugar, helped by the green material chlorophyll. Curled dehydrated leaves cannot do this well.

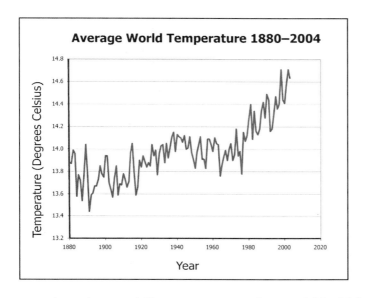

Use the internet. Collect facts to support your answer.

- What happened to the world's temperature from 1880–2004?

- Discuss the three solutions for food crops below with your group.
- Write notes so that you can report to the class.

1. Grow the crop farther north where the climate is cooler.	2. Grow the crop on higher ground where the climate is cooler.	3. Find ways to change the plants so that they can cope with higher temperatures.

Possible solution	
Advantages	**Disadvantages**

ECO World Savers

Teacher's Guide & Planning

The Key Issues

- Global rainfall patterns are changing: temperate regions are becoming wetter and sub-tropical regions drier.
- Changes in rainfall patterns affect crops, livestock and people.

Additional Activities

Language

- Research and write a newspaper article about how changing rainfall patterns could affect the local area and its inhabitants. Include suggestions as to what action might be needed. Include photographs, maps and charts, using computer software.

Maths

- Make accurate measurements and calculations of liquid volume/capacity.

Science

- Learn about the water-cycle and investigate evaporation and condensation. Provide cans containing ice and ask the children to observe, record and explain what happens to the outside of the can, then to plan investigations to check their explanations.

Geography

- Set up a weather station, measure and record rainfall and store the data using graphing software. Begin a long-term record of local weather and make comparisons with any previous records. Use email to exchange local weather information with schools in other regions and countries.

Research

- Find out what different scientists are saying about the causes and effects of rainfall change, and the evidence.
- Use the internet to find out which countries are likely to be the most adversely affected by changing rainfall patterns and what they are doing to deal with its causes and the effects.

More Information

The quantity of water in the Earth and its atmosphere remains constant but its distribution changes. Water is constantly being absorbed by air, falling to the ground as precipitation (rain, snow, hail), running off impermeable surfaces, soaking through permeable ones, collecting underground, flowing in streams and rivers to lakes and the sea and evaporating into the air. Factors such as temperature, wind, tides, gasses in the air and disturbances such as earthquakes and volcanoes affect this cycle. Scientists are observing and measuring the effects of human activity, such as fossil-fuel burning, on the water cycle. A useful website is www.worldclimate.com.

PROTECTING OUR FOOD AND WATER SUPPLY
Too Dry

Scientists at Environment Canada investigated rainfall from 1925 to 1999. They found that rainfall *increased* in northern Europe, Canada and northern Russia but *decreased* in large areas of southern India, Southeast Asia and Africa south of the Sahara desert.

- Use the internet to find the average yearly rainfall for the countries or regions listed on the chart.
- Find the countries or regions on a globe or world map.
- What is happening to the rainfall there?
- What might it be like there in ten years' time?
- How will this affect crops, livestock and people?

Country or region	Is the rainfall increasing (I) or decreasing (D)?	What it might be like in ten years	Effect on crops, livestock and people
Canada			
Southern India			
Namibia			
Northern Russia			
Zimbabwe			
Philippines			
Southern China			
Norway			
France			
United Kingdom			

ECO World Savers

Teacher's Guide & Planning

The Key Issues

- Bare land becomes vulnerable to accelerated erosion.
- Severe wind and rain increase erosion.

Additional Activities

Language and ICT

- Use a computer to produce reports, with photographs, maps and charts, about soil erosion and preventing it.
- Collect examples of verbs that form nouns following the same pattern as erode/erosion: corrode/corrosion, explode/explosion, decide/decision.

Maths and Science

- Investigate ideas for preventing erosion while young plants are growing: for example, by creating wind-breaks and barriers to prevent water erosion.
- Take this opportunity to practise weighing and measuring with precision and recoding data using graphs and charts (by hand or using graphing software).

Geography

- Find out about places with soil erosion through loss of vegetation, where crops cannot easily be grown: Easter Island, Iceland, Orkney, deserts. Look at climate details and what inhibits vegetation recovery: very high/low temperatures, low rainfall and so on.
- Look at terraced slopes: tea-plantations in Sri Lanka. Adapt the investigation on page 9 to test the effects of terracing on erosion.

Research

- Use the internet to find data on the sizes of deserts over the years. Describe what has happened: for example, whether their area has increased or decreased.
- Read Dr Ray Weil's illustrated recount of soil erosion in Ethiopia. Identify the key points makes. Link this with work in science by repeating his experiment. See http://soil.gsfc.nasa.gov/stories/erosion.htm

---

More Information

Background erosion is a natural process that removes soil at about the same rate as it is formed. Accelerated erosion is loss of soil at a much faster rate than it is formed. It is the result of human action such as overgrazing or inappropriate cultivation methods (including powerful agricultural implements). These make the soil vulnerable to rain and wind, which detach the soil and move it to other locations. Accelerated erosion affects cultivated and uncultivated areas, causing problems at the erosion site and deposit site.

Most food crops need soil. In some places soil is being eroded (washed or blown away).

- Find out how this happens. Try this:

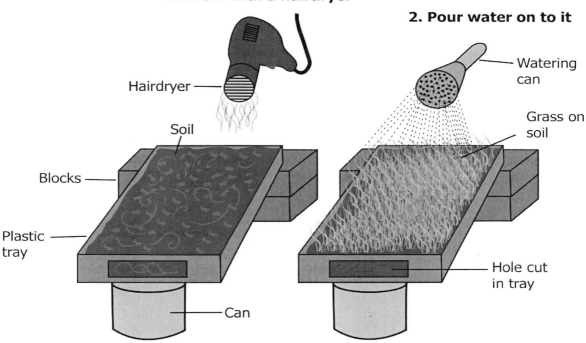

1. Blow with a hairdryer

Hairdryer

Soil

Blocks

Plastic tray

Can

2. Pour water on to it

Watering can

Grass on soil

Hole cut in tray

- What happens when rain lands on sloping ground?
- What difference do plants make?
- What happens if you make the slope steeper?
- Record your results on a chart:

Height of top of slope (cm)	Amount of soil blown away (g)		Amount of soil washed away (g)	
	Grass	**No grass**	**Grass**	**No grass**

Think about:
- how to look after land with no crops.
- how to alter the slope of land.

- What can be done to stop rain and wind eroding soil?

PROTECTING OUR FOOD AND WATER SUPPLY
Busy Bees

Teacher's Guide & Planning

The Key Issues

- Flowering plants need to be pollinated in order to produce seeds.
- Many flowering plants are pollinated by insects such as bees.
- World bee populations are falling.

Additional Activities

Language

- Read novels such as *Animal Farm* by George Orwell or *Watership Down* by Richard Adams to find out how authors use animal characters to communicate a message. Write a story set in a hive with the queen, drones and workers as characters.

Science and ICT

- Make photographs and drawings of flowers then describe how they attract insects and ensure that pollen rubs off onto them: perfume, bright colours, a trumpet-shaped flower (broom, daffodil, antirrhinum), 'honey guides' (target-like patterns: daisy, lily, dandelion), a platform-like structure for insects to land on (yarrow and sedum).

Art and Humanities

- Make large multi-media collages or three-dimensional models of bees and other pollinating insects.
- Explore musical instruments and sound-makers to represent the sounds or movements of insects. Use simple notation to record this.

Research

- Use information books, CD-ROMs and the internet to find out about other insects that pollinate plants: butterflies, moths and hoverflies.
- Read what scientists say about the decline of the world bee population, the causes and solutions. See the websites of national bee-keeping associations.
- Invite a bee-keeper to talk about caring for bees and harvesting honey.

More Information

Worker honey bees and bumble bees visit flowers to collect nectar and pollen to feed the hive. A long tongue unfolds to lap up nectar. This is stored internally, in the bee's crop. It is regurgitated in the hive and stored in wax cells made by workers. As the bee collects nectar, pollen collects on hairs on its head, body and legs. Most falls into 'pollen baskets' on its legs but some rubs off onto the stigmas of flowers. Pollen grains move down the stigma to the ovary, where they fertilise ovules. These grow into seeds. Some plants are self-pollinating; others need pollen from another plant of the same species.

- Read the notes to find out about pollination.
- What happens in each part of the plant?
- What does the bee do?
- Write in the boxes.

Pollination

Ovules grow in ovary (female part of flowers)

To grow into seeds ovules need pollen

Pollen is on anthers (tips of stamens-male parts of flowers)

Pollen has to get from stamens to stigma (top of ovary)

Pollen goes down tubes in ovary to reach ovules

Pollen fertilises ovules

Ovules grow into seeds.

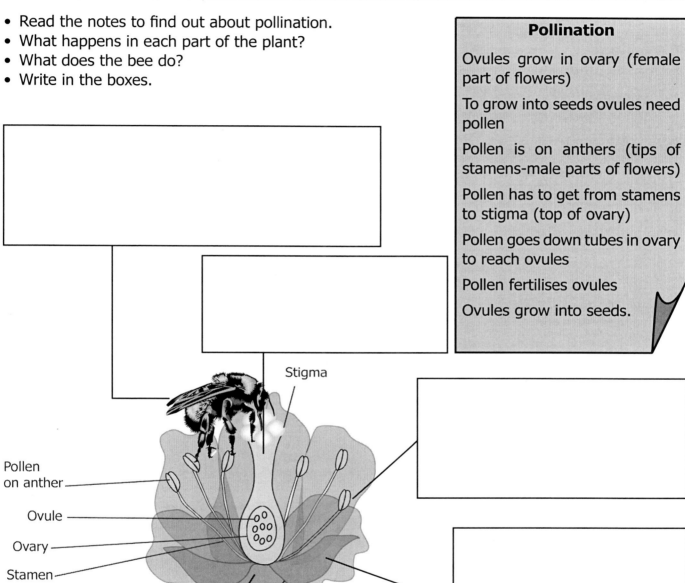

Stigma

Pollen on anther

Ovule

Ovary

Stamen

Petal

ECO World Savers

PROTECTING OUR FOOD AND WATER SUPPLY
A World Of Meat Eaters

Teacher's Guide & Planning

The Key Issues

- Overall world meat consumption is increasing, especially in countries whose economy is growing fast.
- To meet the demand for meat industrial farming, in which animals are kept indoors, is increasing.

Additional Activities

Language

- After researching industrial farming methods list their advantages and disadvantages (and for whom). Hold a debate about whether animals should be reared indoors for food.
- Write and perform a play with 'free range' and 'battery' animals as the main characters. Alternatively, this could be written as a picture story or play for younger children.

Religious education

- Explore religious dietary laws or preferences and the reasons: the scriptures, tradition, local availability. Prepare and eat foods associated with a religion.

Art and Humanities

- Find explanations for changes in farming in the past and consider the social reasons: for example, the rise in sheep-farming in 16th century England and 18th–19th century Scotland, the development of wheat farming in 18th–19th century Canada, beef production in 19th century Brazil or sugar in the Caribbean, and their links with slavery.
- Look at maps showing agricultural land in a specific country. Identify physical and human features that favour particular types of agriculture.

Research

- Visit a farm to learn about the care and management of livestock, also find out about humane slaughter.
- Find out about changing meat production and consumption in different countries.

More Information

Animals need air, water, food and shelter, all of which can be provided indoors. National regulations on animal welfare vary with respect to the minimum space per animal. Waste from animals kept indoors has to be disposed of safely. It can be used as fertiliser but transport from cities to rural farmland can be difficult and costly. Views on aspects of animal well-being, such as quality of life, vary. As economies develop, populations become wealthier and can afford more meat: from 1960 to 1990 meat consumption in Japan increased 360%.

ECO World Savers

PROTECTING OUR FOOD AND WATER SUPPLY
A World Of Meat Eaters

More and more livestock (poultry, pigs and cattle) are being kept in 'landless' industrial farms run by large industrial businesses.

- List the needs of each animal.
- Make notes about how these needs might be met in landless industrial farms.
- Make notes about any problems that might arise.

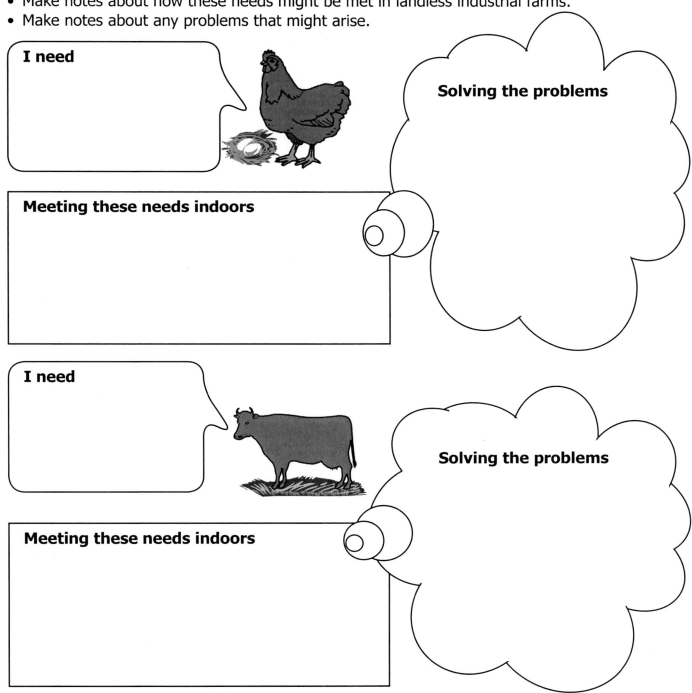

I need

Meeting these needs indoors

Solving the problems

I need

Meeting these needs indoors

Solving the problems

ECO World Savers

Teacher's Guide & Planning

The Key Issues

- Humans compete with other organisms for food.
- Scientists have found ways to increase crops' disease resistance and vulnerability to insect attack: including genetic modification.
- Some pesticides can cause harm to humans and other animals.

Additional Activities

Language

- Read poetry to explore ideas about farming issues: 'Thistles' (Karla Kuskin), 'Harvest Hymn' (John Betjeman) and 'Chromosome Poem' (J Patrick Lewis).

Science and ICT

- Explore food chains and webs to establish that food chains start with a plant. Use computer software to build up food webs for other crops. Discuss ways of using predator/prey relationships to protect plants without pesticides: for example, ladybirds, which do *not* harm plants, feed on greenfly and some mildews, which *do*.
- Provide pictures, with captions, of plants and animals from a food web and ask the children to use information texts to help them to construct the web.

Art

- Make 'food chain' mobiles with two- or three-dimensional models of living things suspended in the correct order for their food chain.

Research

- Research the banning of pesticides: arsenic and copper compounds used in the nineteenth century and DDT and organo-phosphates in the twentieth century.
- Investigate organic crop protection, from window boxes and gardens to farms
- Find out about genetic engineering, which is not new but less precise than modern methods. Traditional breeding manipulates genes indirectly. Genetic engineering alters genes directly using molecular cloning and transformation.

More Information

Many of the world's poor have not benefited from increased food growing policies because they are too poor. Many farmers cannot afford the chemicals and improved seeds to increase crop yields. Scientists now refer to 'The Gene Revolution' which uses biotechnology to create new **genetically modified** (GM) crops. These can produce more food with fewer chemicals than traditional crops. But there is some argument about whether these crops are safe to eat and could threaten the environment. Many question whether government agencies test the products enough. The big debate is: Are GM crops safe and environmentally friendly or an out-of-control experiment?

PROTECTING OUR FOOD AND WATER SUPPLY
Bugs And Blights

- Look at the food chain below. Complete the chart.

• List five organisms that feed on lettuce.	• Choose a lettuce-eater. Find out how to control it organically. Write notes.
• What would happen to the organisms in the food web if the farmer put slug pellets around the lettuce?	
• What would happen to the organisms if the farmer sprayed the lettuce with a fungicide?	

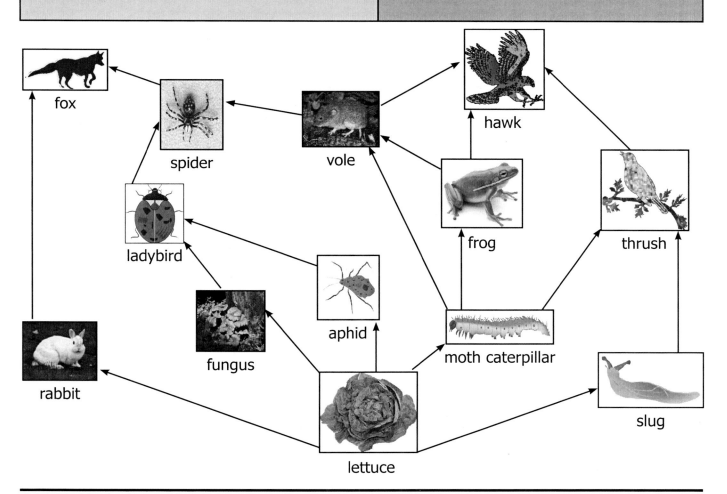

fox

spider

vole

hawk

ladybird

frog

thrush

fungus

aphid

moth caterpillar

rabbit

slug

lettuce

ECO World Savers

Teacher's Guide & Planning

The Key Issues

- Biomass fuels are made from living things or the waste they produce.
- Many biomass fuels come from plants that can also be grown as food crops.
- Growing crops for fuel could lead to a shortage of land for food crops and livestock.

Additional Activities

Language

- Use a table in a computer program to organise a glossary of words with the prefix bio- (from Greek *bios*, meaning life). Predict the meanings before looking them up.

Science

- Construct electrical circuits using electricity produced in different ways: for example, using a hand-generator or solar cells. Use the electricity to produce light.
- Grow small amounts of biofuel crops such as maize, sunflowers, soya and miscanthus.

Geography

- Consider advantages and disadvantages of biomass fuel crops: they might reduce carbon emissions by replacing fossil fuels. But some scientists say that if they are not grown in a sustainable way they could produce *more* carbon dioxide than fossil fuels. They could also take over land used for food crops or livestock.

Research

- Research different views about biofuels. Discuss evidence to compare the carbon emissions produced during growing and manufacture. Compare this with carbon emissions from petroleum-based fuels.
- Carry out a survey of domestic fuels used locally. Use graphing software to record and present the results.

More Information

All the plants shown in the pictures can be used for fuel. Biomass fuels include: wood, wood chippings, straw, pellets or liquids made from wood, biogas (methane) from human or other animal waste and ethanol, diesel or other liquid fuels made from plant material or waste oil. Ethanol for fuel is made through fermentation, as in wine and beer. Biodiesel is made using various chemical processes. Bio-ethanol can be mixed with petrol. Biodiesel can be used on its own or in a mixture. Useful websites: Friends of the Earth (www.foei.org), Greenpeace (www.greenpeace.org).

PROTECTING OUR FOOD AND WATER SUPPLY
Crops For Burning

- Can these be used for fuel? Discuss this with your group.
- Write yes or no.
- Use information books and the internet to check your answers.
- Write notes about one that surprised you. Tell another group about it.

Soya

Palm oil

Sugar cane

Maize

Oilseed rape

Sunflower oil

Fuel:

Notes:

Where is it grown? How is it made into fuel? How is it used?

PROTECTING OUR FOOD AND WATER SUPPLY
Not Just For Breakfast

Teacher's Guide & Planning

The Key Issues

- Wheat and rice crops in many places are failing because of drought, severe winds, floods and a rise in diseases. This leads to price increases.
- Many foods that we take for granted are made from wheat or rice.
- Many poor people in rural areas of developing countries could face starvation because their diets rely mainly on wheat or rice.

Additional Activities

Language

- After discussing the causes of rice and wheat price rises and who gains and loses, write poems to express opinions. Encourage the use of questions and answers and words that have evocative connotations and sounds: for example, to evoke anger, sadness, despair, greed.

Science

- Grow small areas of wheat and rice (as small as one square metre), or sow a few seeds indoors and try to replicate the ideal growing conditions. Record their growth and any problems that hamper this. You could even harvest wheat from a tiny plot and mill it to make flour.

Humanities

- Look at world maps showing agriculture to find out about the main crops of different countries. Compare recent maps with those from ten or twenty years ago.

Research

- Find out about the staple foods of different areas and communities and how they might cope with shortages, including the work of aid organisations: www.oxfam.org, www.unicef.org, www.islamic-relief.com, www.savethechildren.org

---

More Information

Almost everyone eats at least one of the five leading staple foods on a regular basis, as long as they are available: wheat, rice, corn (maize), potatoes or cassava. When the major world producers' crops are reduced through severe weather or shortages due to increased biofuel growing, poor rural communities, who cannot easily find alternative foods, are affected severely. For many people the main problem is increased prices. In the year up to March 2008 World wheat prices rose by 130%, soya by 57%, corn by 31% (Bloomberg) and rice by 74% (Jackson Sons & Co). According to Food and Agriculture Organisation of the United Nations (www.fao.org/) estimates, 923 million people in the world are undernourished and that high prices are the cause for 75 million of these.

PROTECTING OUR FOOD AND WATER SUPPLY
Not Just For Breakfast

If the world's rice and wheat crops failed because of disease and severe weather, how would your diet change?

- Keep a food diary for a week.
- Draw a line through the foods that you would not have.
- Write your ideas about what you would eat instead.

Food diary	
Monday _____	**Thursday** _____
_____	_____
_____	_____
Tuesday _____	**Friday** _____
_____	_____
_____	_____
Wednesday _____	**Saturday** _____
_____	
_____	**Sunday** _____
_____	_____
_____	_____

Other carbohydrate foods I could eat

Rice and wheat are carbohydrates. They give us energy.

_____

ECO World Savers

PROTECTING OUR FOOD AND WATER SUPPLY
Fish Harvest

Teacher's Guide & Planning

The Key Issues

- As capture fishing methods become more and more efficient they could destroy the very fish stock they depend on.
- Depleted fishing grounds recover very slowly, if at all.
- Breeding grounds can be protected.

Additional Activities

Language

- Write stories about *The Last Fish* using the storyline to communicate the message that if people continue catching fish from the sea and from lakes without taking action to ensure that the different species survive there could well be no more fish to catch.

Maths and Science

- Investigate the life-cycles of fish, especially those that travel to specific breeding grounds.
- Compare respiration in fish with that of land animals.
- Look up the food values of different species of fish and compare fish to other protein sources.
- Make scale drawings of commonly-eaten fish for comparison: for example tuna, mackerel, sardine, cod, plaice, sea bass.

Art and Humanities

- Use books and the internet to help in a case-study of an area whose fish stock have been, or are, depleted, for example, whales in Antarctica.

Research

- Use internet sources and, if possible, surveys with small- and large-scale fishers to find out how well they make a livelihood from fishing and what they do (voluntarily and because of legislation) to sustain the fishing grounds they depend on.
- Find out about the place of cod in the food chain in the seas around Newfoundland.

More Information

According to the Food and Agriculture Organisation of the United Nations, capture (ie non-farmed fishing) fishing production decreased from 93.2 million tonnes in 2002 to 92 million tonnes in 2006. However, inland capture fishing increased from 8.7 to 10.1 million tonnes in the same period and, if aquaculture is taken into account, overall fish production increased from 89.3 to 143.6 million tonnes. The same source showed that China was by far the greatest producer. See *The State of World Fisheries and Aquaculture* www.fao.org.

- Discuss the story of the Newfoundland fisheries with your group.
- Write your ideas about what caused the problem.
- What can we learn from this?

Time-line

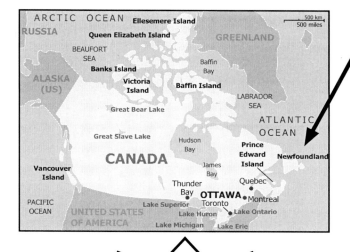

	Time-line
Indigenous people fish in seas round Newfoundland. Huge numbers of fish.	**2000 BCE or earlier**
Viking explorers build settlement near coast, where they fish.	**1000 CE**
Explorer John Cabot: 'You can lower a basket into the sea and pull it up full of cod'.	**1647**
Fishers from Europe, using lines – regular trips. Salt fish for long journey back.	**1750**
Huge factory ships from distant places with sonar systems to find fish. Trawl nets drag along seabed – disturb breeding habitats. Factory ships freeze fish at sea to keep fresh on long journey back.	**1950s**
Big local investment in fishing industry. Fishers notice fewer fish in sea.	**1980s**
No cod in the sea.	**1992**

Causes

What we can learn

ECO World Savers

Teacher's Guide & Planning

The Key Issues

- Overall global fish consumption is on the rise.
- Aquaculture (fish farming) has increased in order to meet world demands for fish.
- Feeding farmed carnivorous fish on meal made from small fish uses more of these small fish than if they were used for human consumption.

Additional Activities

Language

- Hold a debate about fish farming: different groups could plan speeches that support or oppose it, giving researched reasons. Groups can organise their work so that different members research different aspects.

Maths and Science

- Trout (or other river fish) eggs can be bought and reared in suitable tanks of running water. This can be set up using a plastic tank placed beneath a dripping tap and with an outlet pipe covered with fine gauze to prevent eggs escaping. The local water company might provide the eggs and give advice on releasing the young fish into rivers.

Art and Humanities

- Carry out a case-study of a place where a sea, lake or river fish farm has been set up. Find out how this has affected the area: the water, shore or banks, employment, population movement (including immigration), transport and buildings.

Research

- Find out how animal welfare organisations are campaigning for the welfare of farmed fish. Find out what they have achieved so far and how this affects fish farmers.
- Research the problems caused by escaping farmed fish: how they can spread disease and how interbreeding with wild fish can affect the future of the species. Find out about actions that can reduce these problems.

More Information

According to the Food and Agriculture Organisation of the United Nations, in 2006 aquaculture accounted for 17.2 million tonnes of global fish production and utilisation, excluding that of China. Problems facing fish farms include feeding a diet that meets all the nutritional needs without harming stocks of other fish or the environment, the control of diseases, which can spread rapidly among large numbers of fish kept in one place and ensuring that the fish remain free of materials harmful to the people who eat them.

- Use the salmon-farming facts to help you to write an argument about salmon farming.

A report in the journal *Science* said that 90 per cent of the world's fisheries could be over-fished within 40 years.

Popular fish, such as salmon, can be reared in great numbers in fish farms.

Fish farmers are investigating fish foods made from plants, such as soya.

Farmed carnivorous fish, such as salmon, cod, sea bass and sea bream are fed fishmeal pellets made from edible wild fish such as pilchard. It can take more than three kilos of these to produce a kilogram of salmon.

Wild salmon feed on shrimp and krill, which give the flesh a deep pink colour. Fish feed does not contain enough pigment to give the fish the colour people like, so they are fed a food additive called canthaxanthin (E161g).

Carnivorous fish can not survive on plant-based feeds alone.

Farmed salmon reach their adult weight much more quickly than wild ones.

Farmed salmon are starved for about seven days before harvesting in order to clear the digestive system of feed, which could affect freshness. This does not happen in wild fish.

The main pigments used by most fish farmers are artificially produced but, chemically, they are the same as natural pigments.

Is salmon-farming a good thing?

ECO World Savers

Teacher's Guide & Planning

The Key Issues

- Every stage of food production relies on fossil fuels.
- If world oil supplies ran out developed countries could suffer famine.

Additional Activities

Language Writing

- Contact schools (write, email, fax and/or text) in other places to compare findings about local produce. Write reports.
- Decide how the school and its locality could help to reduce oil consumption: for example, stopping the use of plastic bags, turning electrical devices off 'standby', walking to school or using public transport instead of the car (or car-sharing).

Maths and Science

- Use the OPEC website to check oil prices each day; interpret data in graphs and charts. Notice trends and look for explanations.
- Calculate 'shopping basket' prices of foods bought on a regular basis to compare the prices of organic with other foods.
- Find out the origins of foods in the 'shopping basket' for organic and other foods add up the total miles it has travelled.

Art and Humanities Geography

- Compare two oil-producing regions: growth of cities, roads and other transport, and population changes and movement.
- Visit a farmers' market and find out about local produce and how far it has travelled. Compare this with similar supermarket items.
- Use maps to trace the routes travelled by foods that are grown, produced, processed and packed in different places.

Research

- Find out which countries produce oil and about OPEC (Organisation of the Petroleum Exporting Countries, www.opec.org).
- Compare organic with other farming methods to find out to what extent it affects dependency on oil, taking into consideration the use of chemicals and any differences in transport distances.

More Information

Oil is used at every stage of food production: to power farm machinery, in the production of fertilisers and pesticides (raw materials and running machinery), in processing, packaging (for the products themselves and running the machinery to produce them and pack the food) and in creating and maintaining the infrastructure for production, storage, transport and selling. Cheap energy takes the place of manual labour. Buying locally-produced foods, thus buying seasonally, helps to reduce oil consumption.

PROTECTING OUR FOOD AND WATER SUPPLY
Eating Oil

- How are oil and other fossil fuels used in food production?
- Discuss these with your group and write your answers.

Farming

Food processing: bread, biscuits ready meals, cakes and so on

Packaging

Transport

Shopping

ECO World Savers

PROTECTING OUR FOOD AND WATER SUPPLY
Waste Wise

Teacher's Guide & Planning

The Key Issues

- The average household in many developed countries throws away about a third of the food it buys.
- Waste can be reduced by planning – buying only what is needed, improving knowledge about storage and labelling and improving cooking skills, especially in using leftover food and 'store cupboard' items.

Additional Activities

Language

- Read the labels on food packaging and look up anything that is not understood: for example, 'sell by', 'use by' and 'best before' dates, symbols and ingredients, including additives.
- Create a glossary of food words, including additives, words used on packaging, alternative names for foods, unfamiliar foods.

Maths and Science

- Plan a week's recipes to include foods of different types (proteins, fats, carbohydrates as well as fruit and vegetables). Calculate the amounts of each food required for, say, four people, and write a shopping list. Use supermarket websites to find the prices. Discuss and list anything that would be left over and whether it could be stored or used up: for example, onion, broccoli stalks and potato for making soup that can be frozen.

Art and Humanities

- Use different sources (the internet, holiday photographs and memories, books, leaflets) to find out how people living in rural areas in developing countries buy, store and use food, particularly hot places where poor people have no refrigeration. Compare this with their own experiences.

Research

- Find out about food waste statistics for different countries. Note the main types of food thrown away, consider why and what could be done to reduce this.
- Find out about the rationale behind the activities of 'freegans' (people who raid food stores' bins for discarded food).

More Information

According to the Waste & Resources Action Programme, it is estimated that 6.7 million tonnes of household food waste is produced each year in the UK, most of which could have been eaten. This not only wastes food, but costs us all money and a major contributor to the production of greenhouse gasses. 20% of the UK's greenhouse gas emissions are associated with food production, distribution and storage. If we stopped wasting food, we could prevent about 15 million tonnes of carbon dioxide each year contributing to global warming. Much food waste goes to landfill sites where it decomposes, producing methane – a greenhouse gas 25 times more dangerous than carbon dioxide.

- Carry out a survey of the foods wasted in your home in a week.
- Write on the bins.

- Collect the results of your group or class.
- Record them on the graph.

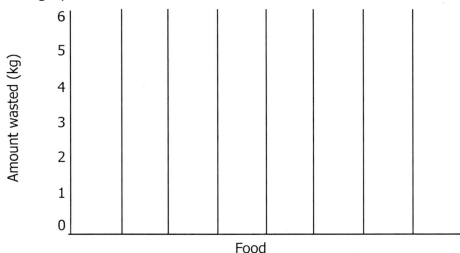

- What kinds of food is the most often wasted? _____

- Explain this _____

_____

ECO World Savers

PROTECTING OUR FOOD AND WATER SUPPLY
Water, Water Everywhere

Teacher's Guide & Planning

The Key Issues

- Water sources can be classed as surface water or groundwater.
- Surface water is water that can be seen in streams, rivers and lakes. It flows on the surface of the ground.
- Groundwater is water that has seeped through porous soil and rock until it reaches an impermeable layer of rock, where it forms an aquifer.

Additional Activities

Language

- Look up words that begin with the Latin prefix *aqua* (sometimes changed as in aquifer, aqueduct) aquamarine, aquatic, aquaculture, aquarium, aqualung.
- Read and discuss *The Well: David's Story* by Mildred Taylor – a family share their well water with neighbours when the other wells in the village run dry.

Maths and Science

- Investigate evaporation: leave measured amounts of water in shallow dishes in different places, measure any remaining water the next day and explain the results. Explore condensation: half-fill shiny cans with ice, describe what happens.
- Draw diagrams of the water cycle and use the results of practical investigations to explain why water rises into the air and what makes it fall again as precipitation (rain, hail or snow).

Art and Humanities

- Take photographs of water. Encourage creativity using digital cameras an then editing software for producing different effects. Produce paintings based on the photographs.

Research

- Find out where the school's water comes from. Contact schools in other countries and regions and share information about local water supplies.
- Find out how the water is collected from different sources: water holes, draw wells, pumped wells, artesian wells, etc. Notice any differences between urban and remote rural water supplies.

More Information

Of the Earth's water 97% is salt water. Of the remaining 3% about 66% is frozen in polar ice caps and glaciers. The remaining fresh water consists mainly of groundwater and a very small amount above ground or in the air.

The water we use at home, school and other places can come from different sources. How does it get there?

• Complete the flow-charts.

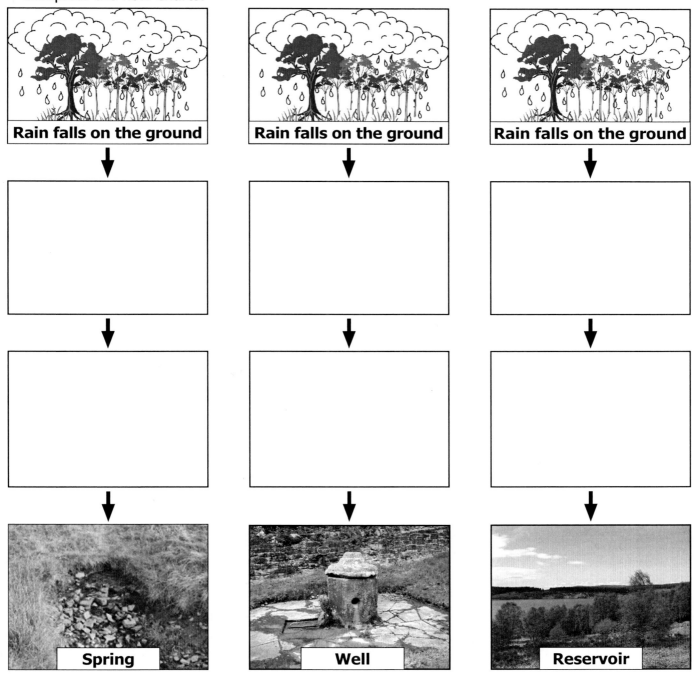

Rain falls on the ground	Rain falls on the ground	Rain falls on the ground
Spring	**Well**	**Reservoir**

• Find out about the source of the water for your home and school.

ECO World Savers

PROTECTING OUR FOOD AND WATER SUPPLY
Running Water

Teacher's Guide & Planning

The Key Issues

- We can not survive without water.
- Most human activity uses water in some way.
- We can avoid wasting water by making small changes.

Additional Activities

Maths

- Measure how much water flows through a garden hose or from a tap into a large container in one minute. Use this to calculate how much water is used for brushing teeth, washing hands under running water, washing a car, watering a garden and so on.
- Use this as an opportunity to consolidate knowledge of capacity and volume and the units for measuring them.

Science and ICT

- Plan and carry out fair tests to find out which types of houseplant need the least and most water.

History

- Compare modern household use of water with that of a previous age, focusing on how and where water was used, and estimating how much.

Geography

- Use the internet to find a local water company's estimates of the amount of water used for various household activities. Also find out their water metering charges.
- Compare typical household water use in rich and poor households in different countries.
- Find out how water is brought from a source to the school and compare this with a contrasting location.

Research

- Carry out a survey on water use in school: list the different ways in which it is used and find ways to measure this: for example, by collecting and measuring the amount of water used for one handwash and then multiplying it by the average number of times people wash their hands. Also use online water calculators, e.g. www.waterfootprint.org.

More Information

According to http://earthtrends.wri.org, the USA used a total of 467.3 km^3 of water (1,834 m^3 per capita) in 1990: 42% for agriculture, 42% for industry and 13% for domestic users. UK total consumption was 11.8 km^3 (204 m^3 per capita): 77% for industry, 3% for agriculture and 20% for domestic users. See also http://water.usgs.gov for other US data. For comparison, total consumption in Kenya was 2 km^3 (87 m^3 per capita).

How is water used at home?
- List as many examples as you can in each category:
- Estimate how much water each one uses.

	Examples	Amount
Eating and drinking		
Personal hygiene		
Household cleaning		
Garden		
Car		
? Other		

- Choose one type of water use.
- Find a way to work out how much is used each week.
- Compare this with your estimate.

ECO World Savers

PROTECTING OUR FOOD AND WATER SUPPLY
Water Footprint

Teacher's Guide & Planning

The Key Issues

- In addition to water that can be seen and measured everyone also uses 'virtual water': all the water that is used in producing food, clothing and other items.
- Total water use can be calculated to assess the 'water footprint' of an individual, family, business, other organisation, city or country.

Additional Activities

Language

- Write and present persuasive speeches to make an audience aware of the virtual water they use and their water footprints, and how these affect people in countries where there are water shortages. Link this with audio/visual effects produced in art/ICT lessons.
- Write letters to a local council to find out about its water footprint and what it is doing to reduce it.

Maths and Science

- Calculate individual, family and school water footprints.
- Compare the water footprints of meat-eaters and vegetarians. Calculate the water saved by substituting some meat-based meals with vegetarian.

Art and Humanities

- Use the internet to find out and compare the water footprints of a developing and developed country and discuss how fair this is in the use of global resources.
- Design graphics to illustrate the 'virtual water' used in producing different foods and clothing.
- Use art software to create audio and visual effects to enhance a message about water consumption.

Research

- Find out about the extent to which developed countries are affecting water supplies in developing countries, especially those where inhabitants face problems due to water shortages.

More Information

Volumes of water used in producing the raw materials for the items depicted, for processing, packing and transporting them amount to approximately: leather shoes 8,000 litres, 500 g of beef 8,000 litres, cotton shirt 2,900 litres, hamburger 2,300 litres, 500 g of rice 1,150 litres, 1 litre of milk 800 litres, a 35 ml can of cola 200 litres, a cup of black coffee 140 litres. This is known as 'virtual water'. It can be used to assess the 'water footprint' of a person or organisation. An individual's water footprint can be calculated on www.waterfootprint.org.

PROTECTING OUR FOOD AND WATER SUPPLY
Water Footprint

- Work in a group.
- Which of these use the most water to produce?
- List the food and clothing in order.
- Explain your answer.

500 g of beef

a pair of leather shoes

a cotton shirt

a 35 ml can of cola

500 g of rice

a litre of milk

a cup of black coffee

a hamburger

		Item	Explanation
Most water	1		
	2		
	3		
	4		
	5		
	6		
	7		
Least water	8		

Teacher's Guide & Planning

The Key Issues

- Humans and most other land animals, as well as most food crops, need fresh water.
- Salt can be removed from water by evaporating and then condensing the water, leaving the salt behind and collecting the fresh condensed water.

Additional Activities

Language

- Use this as an opportunity to explore words that have the prefix de- with the same meaning as in desalinate ('take away'). Examples include debug, decaffeinate, defrost, demist, deodorant.

Maths and Science

- Dissolve salt in water and find ways of separating the two so that the salt or water is collected. Discuss what energy sources are used: for example, the sun's heat, gas, electricity.
- Grow crystals from a saturated solution of salt or sugar: heat the water, add solute; keep stirring until no more will dissolve; pour into clean jar; suspend a thread in the solution with a paperclip as a weight; leave in a warm place. Crystals will grow on the thread.

Art and Humanities

- Design and make salt and sugar crystal gardens by adding food colourings to the solutions.
- Compare and explain the main water sources of two contrasting countries.

Research

- Find out about global use of desalination: which countries use it and why some desert areas make less use of it, if any. This could involve finding out about costs, the relative wealth of the countries studied and their power supplies and other infrastructure.
- Use information from the internet to help to decide whether desalination is ago do way to solve global water shortages.

More Information

Salt water can be desalinated through different processes, all of which involve evaporation and condensation in some form. These involve huge amounts of energy and so are much more costly than other water purification processes. In the Middle East, where fresh water is scarce, it accounted for almost 75% of world desalination. The largest desalination plant in the world is at Jebel Ali in the United Arab Emirates. It can produce 300 million cubic metres of water per year.

PROTECTING OUR FOOD AND WATER SUPPLY
Not A Drop To Drink?

This is a desalination plant. It has its own gas turbine station and there is an overhead line to provide a second supply of electricity.

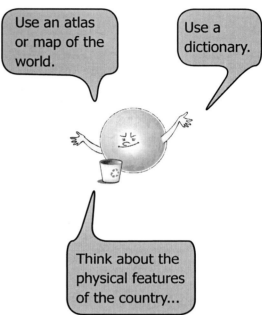

Use an atlas or map of the world.

Use a dictionary.

Think about the physical features of the country...

- What does desalination mean? _____
- What are the main materials used? _____

_____

- Why is desalination important in desert areas? _____
- Name four countries where desalination would be useful.
- What might make it possible there?

Country	Why desalination would be useful	What might make it possible

Teacher's Guide & Planning

The Key Issues

- Air is continually absorbing evaporated water and releasing it as condensation.
- The amount of water per cm^3 of air (the humidity) varies, depending on factors such as temperature, height above sea level, movement of the air.

Additional Activities

Language

- Write reports about how the solar still was set up and what happened. Write explanations about how this happened – where the water in the bowl came from, whether it was fit to drink, and why.

Maths and Science

- Investigate plants from desert habitats: how their structure and life-cycles help them to survive: for example, storing water in thick stems and leaves.
- Grow different plants in hot dry conditions, note which survive, and explain why.

Art and Humanities

- Find out about a desert area, and how people survive there, particularly where their water supplies come from and how water is collected, purified, if necessary, and conserved. Also find out how the lifestyles of the inhabitants are affected by the climate.

Research

- Visit a zoo to look at desert animals. List the features that help them to survive: for example, storage of fat (as in a camel's hump), tough leathery skin for protection from extreme heat in the day (and extreme cold at night), spreading feet for stability on sand.
- Find out how desert animals use features of the habitat to help them to survive.

More Information

Digging a hole helps to create a damp area; water in the earth in the hole evaporates into the air under the polythene. The sun heats the polythene, which creates a small 'greenhouse'. The air inside the hole becomes hotter than the air outside it and droplets of water from the air begin to condense on the underside of the sheet of polythene, as on a window. These water droplets are pure water, fit to drink, because when water containing dissolved materials evaporates it leaves these behind. The stone pushes the polythene downwards, making the droplets drip into the bowl. The only energy used comes from the heat of the sun.

- Make a solar still to collect water:

1. Dig a round hole.

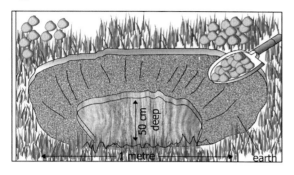

You need:

- a small spade or trowel
- a large bowl
- stones
- a sack of leaves or grass cuttings
- a sheet of polythene about 120 x 120 cm (4ft x 4ft)

2. Put a bowl in the hole.

3. Pack leaves or grass cuttings around the bowl up to just below the top.

4. Put a sheet of polythene over the hole. Weight it with stones.

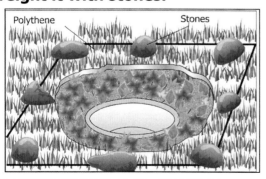

5. Put a small stone in the centre of the polythene to make it dip.

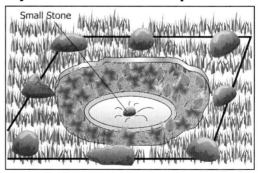

- Describe what happens.
- Explain how this happens.

Teacher's Guide & Planning

The Key Issues

- Most human activity leads to water pollution.
- Materials from some sources are more likely to pollute surface water; others are more likely to pollute ground water.
- Some pollutants have very long-term effects.

Additional Activities

Language

- Write fact-sheets about the sources of water pollution. Different groups could focus on different sources or materials.

Maths and Science

- Compare the life-needs of algae with those of other living things and find out why algae thrive in water polluted by nutrients from farm run-off and how they affect other forms of aquatic life.
- Have a pond-dipping session in which pond animals are observed, photographed for later identification and returned safely to their habitat.

Art and Humanities

- Visit a water treatment plant to find out how pollutants are removed from water supplies – and which ones are difficult or impossible to remove.

Research

- Carry out a survey of local activities that can pollute water and find out how this is being prevented or reduced; for example, how a car-wash disposes of its waste water.
- Use the internet to find out about the various types of water pollution.

More Information

All the items shown can pollute water: (farms) run-off containing ammonia, nitrates, other chemicals and antibiotics in animal waste (surface water and seepage into groundwater), see www.nrdc.org/water/pollution/ffarms.asp; (washing machine) phosphates from detergents enter surface water even after treatment at sewage plants, (nuclear power station) radioactive waste can leak from disposal sites (ground and surface water); (street) run-off into drains contains chemicals from traffic, and can enter surface and ground water; (toilet) human waste is treated and made harmless but viruses from people with illnesses such as hepatitis, typhoid, and cholera can enter surface water, also chemicals from cleaning materials;(rain) heavy rain can cause flooding that leads to sewage entering storm drains; (television set) chemicals from manufacturing as well as disposal of old equipment (surface water and seepage into aquifers); (factory) chemical waste (surface water and seepage into aquifers).

PROTECTING OUR FOOD AND WATER SUPPLY
Water Threats

- Which of these pollute surface or ground water sources?
- Explain your answers.

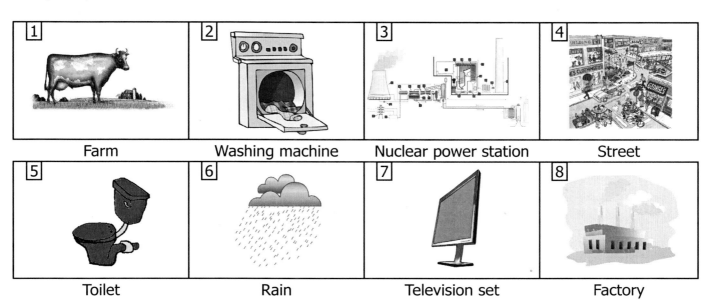

| 1 Farm | 2 Washing machine | 3 Nuclear power station | 4 Street |
| 5 Toilet | 6 Rain | 7 Television set | 8 Factory |

Item	Surface, ground or no pollution	How it pollutes or why it does not pollute
1		
2		
3		
4		
5		
6		
7		
8		

ECO World Savers

PROTECTING OUR FOOD AND WATER SUPPLY
Fit To Drink

Teacher's Guide & Planning

The Key Issues

- Most of the drinking water provided by large water companies in the USA and UK is from groundwater sources: rivers, lakes and reservoirs.
- Groundwater needs to be purified before it is safe to drink.

Additional Activities

Language

- Write explanations of parts of the water purification process for a class poster or booklet.
- Write glossaries of technical and scientific terms such as alum, filtration, floc, micro-organism.
- Write reports based on findings from history or geography lessons.

Maths and Science

- Investigate ways of removing mud and grit from dirty water: pour the water through a filter paper in a funnel; the same topped with gravel; the same topped with sand. Photograph the starting samples and results for comparison. Note that the 'clean' samples should not be drunk.

Art and Humanities

- Use a map to trace the source of, and route followed by, the school's water supply. Identify potential sources of pollution.
- Find out about the water sources for the local area in the past: for example, springs, wells and streams. Look for evidence, such as old pumps and wells.

Research

- Find out how the local water company treats the water and use email to share information with schools whose water supplies are from different sources: river, reservoir, lake, bore-hole, spring, well.
- Investigate 'hard' and 'soft' water: compare, smell, taste, feel and the lather made using the same amount of water and soap.

More Information

Water companies that treat surface water begin by using grilles to remove leaves and other fairly large debris. They then add alum and other chemicals that form sticky particles (floc) to which smaller debris adheres. These sink to the bottom of the water during sedimentation, and clearer water is taken from above them. This is then filtered through sand, gravel and charcoal to remove smaller particles. The filtered water looks clean but could contain harmful micro-organisms: it is disinfected with chlorine and then stored in a covered tank or reservoir, from where it flows through pipes to where it is needed.

PROTECTING OUR FOOD AND WATER SUPPLY
Fit To Drink

- Write the purpose of each stage in this water company's treatment.

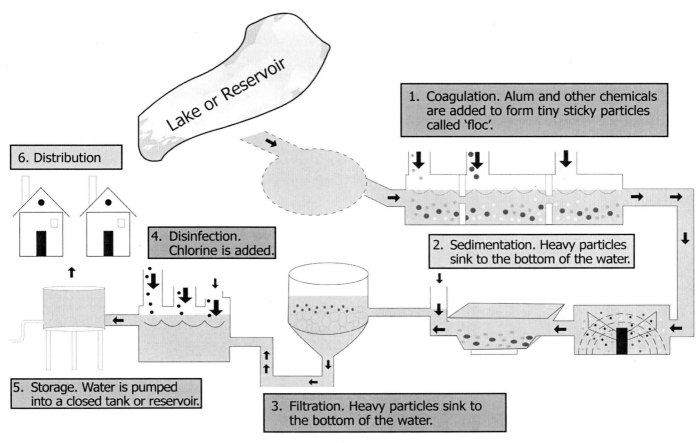

Lake or Reservoir

1. Coagulation. Alum and other chemicals are added to form tiny sticky particles called 'floc'.

6. Distribution

4. Disinfection. Chlorine is added.

2. Sedimentation. Heavy particles sink to the bottom of the water.

5. Storage. Water is pumped into a closed tank or reservoir.

3. Filtration. Heavy particles sink to the bottom of the water.

Stage	Purpose of the treatment
1	
2	
3	
4	
5	
6	

ECO World Savers

Teacher's Guide & Planning

The Key Issues

- If global water supplies are to meet future demands we must use less water.
- We can reduce the amount of water we use for most purposes.

Additional Activities

Language

- Read raps and then use them as models for writing raps about wasted water. Perform a rap written in collaboration with a group to communicate the message to an audience.
- Write and present persuasive speeches about conserving water at home or at school.

Maths and Science

- Use a water meter to measure the amount of water used when taking a shower for 5, 10 and 15 minutes. Compare this with a bath. Measure how much water runs away if the tap is left on while brushing your teeth. Calculate how much would be wasted in a year.
- Measure the amount of water that drips from a tap in five minutes and calculate how much water it could waste in a year.

Art and Humanities

- Find out about the work of charities that help to provide clean water supplies in developing countries and plan a fund-raising initiative to support one of them: for example WaterAid (www.wateraid.org/uk/), www.wateraidamerica.org, www.justadrop.org

Research

- Find out from manufacturers' websites or leaflets how much water is used during different wash cycles of a washing machine or dishwasher. Compare brands.
- Find out about commercially-produced water savers for cisterns: for example, the 'hippo'.
- Use the internet to find out about the ways in which water is wasted, especially through leakage: water companies, domestic, agricultural, industrial.

More Information

Answers: turn off the tap while brushing teeth; shower instead of bath or keep water shallow; run washing machine or dishwasher only when full, use the lowest wash cycle suitable; put a water saver in the toilet cistern, collect rainwater in a water-butt. In your garden, lawns require two-and-a-half to four times more water than shrubs and trees. It is estimated that in the course of a single year, a typical suburban lawn uses 10,000 gallons of water over and above that provided by rainfall.

- How could we save water at home?
- Write your ideas on the notepads.

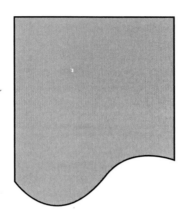

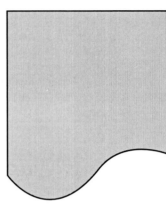

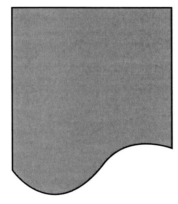
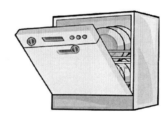

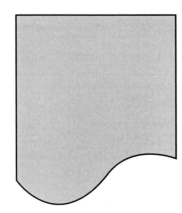

- How can we save water in the garden?

ECO World Savers

Teacher's Guide & Planning

The Key Issues

- Water used for some purposes at home can be re-used.
- This recycled water is known as 'grey water'.
- It can be collected in a bucket or other container or through a 'grey water' system.

Additional Activities

Language

- Read and appraise information texts about water recycling, checking reliability and credentials.
- Write definitions of terms used in water recycling: for example, green water, grey water, black water. Write instructions and warnings connected with water recycling, using information from reliable sources.

Maths and Science

- Compare plants watered with fresh water, grey water and a mixture (alternative fresh and grey).
- Investigate what chemicals are in water, e.g. sodium. Look at the labels on mineral water bottles. Why are these chemicals good for us? Which chemicals would be bad for us?
- Draw a labelled picture of the water cycle. Show how by saving water at home you can influence what happens in this cycle.
- Find out more about developing countries where people may not have clean drinking water.

Art and Humanities

- Collect information about 'grey water' systems, including how the water can be re-used, the risks and the costs and hold a debate about whether these systems should be used.
- Find out about the Blue Lagoon in Iceland, where naturally-occurring minerals and hot water from industry were harnessed to produce a tourist attraction that also has health benefits. (www.bluelagoon.com).

Research

- Find out about industrial grey water schemes, where industries need not use fresh water.

More Information

Waste water from non-toilet plumbing systems such as handbasins, washing machines, showers and baths is known as 'grey water'. Grey water should be used carefully, otherwise it can cause illness to humans and animals and harm plants. Water used for washing crockery, from dishwashers, toilets and bidets is known as 'black water' and should never be re-used. Water recycling should be undertaken with care. A coarse filter can filter out solid material. A professionally-installed system could also treat the grey water. Fresh water (eg collected rainwater) should also be used regularly for watering plants to avoid build-up of salts in the soil.

PROTECTING OUR FOOD AND WATER SUPPLY
Use It Again

• Complete the flow diagram to show which water at home could be recycled and for what purposes.

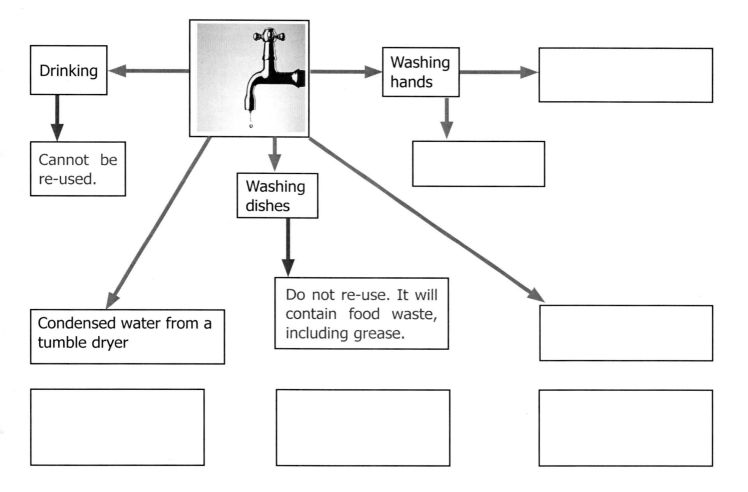

Drinking	Washing hands	

| Cannot be re-used. | | |

| Washing dishes | | |

| Condensed water from a tumble dryer | Do not re-use. It will contain food waste, including grease. | |

• Which water used at home can not be recycled, and why?

Water	Reason for not recycling

ECO World Savers

PROTECTING OUR FOOD AND WATER SUPPLY
Down The Pan

Teacher's Guide & Planning

The Key Issues

- Wherever people live there is waste that has to be removed and made safe.
- Sewage treatment usually involves separating solid and liquid materials and disinfecting the liquid before it can be released into waterways.

Additional Activities

Language

- Write instructions for disposing of sewage, based on what has been learned about different systems. Different groups could write instructions for different systems.

Maths and Science

- Use flow-chart symbols instead of pictures to represent the local sewage disposal system in the form of a flow-chart that shows when a material is removed and when another is added, as well as when different materials take different routes.
- Investigate mixtures of different materials with water: sand and grit, oil, solid fats, leaves, bits of wood and so on. Find ways of separating them stage by stage.

Art and Humanities

- Find out about sewage disposal in cities in the past and about outbreaks of disease caused by contact with sewage. Find out about the first piped sewage systems: for example, in London – but how it affected the water quality of the river Thames and why people left London during the summer.

Research

- Find out about more complex sewage treatments than the one shown in the diagram: for example, where methane gas is removed and used as a fuel or where solid waste is treated and used as a fertiliser.
- Compare the sewage systems of contrasting locations: for example urban and remote rural (which might use septic tanks or reed-beds). Explain how each system ensures that sewage does not pollute fresh water supplies.

More Information

Sewage treatment involves removal of solids by physical screening and sedimentation, and removal of soluble and fine suspended organic pollutants through a type of biological oxidation process. Both of these produce sludge, which is treated and disposed of separately (for example, for sub-soil fertilisation of farmland), and liquid, which is treated to make it safe for disposal in waterways.

ECO World Savers

PROTECTING OUR FOOD AND WATER SUPPLY
Down The Pan

- Describe what happens to sewage from your home.
- Use the diagram and notes to help you to fill in the gaps in the passage.

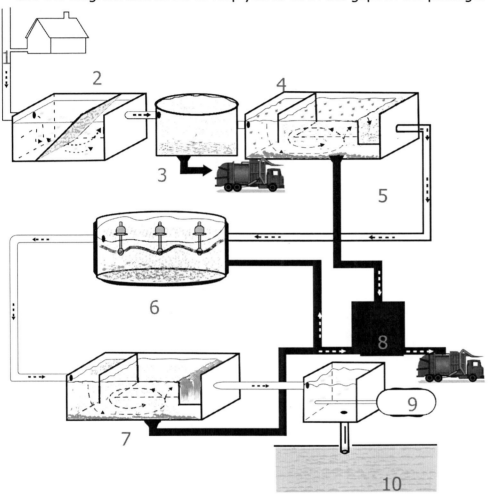

Notes

1 Collection
2 Large items screened out
3 Grit settles and is removed
4 Solids settle
5 Solids removed
6 Aeration: air pumped in
7 Remaining solids settle
8 Solids treated
9 Chlorine added to remaining water to disinfect
10 Clean water to waterways

Sewage from homes flows into a _____ which takes it to the treatment works. First a grille removes _____. The sewage then passes into a tank where _____ settles to the bottom. This is taken away. The sewage still has some solid material in it. This _____ to the bottom of the next tank. A _____ takes them from the bottom of this tank to another _____ where it is _____. Then they are taken away.

Meanwhile, the liquid that is left flows into a tank where _____ is added to it. There are still tiny particles of _____ in it and these _____ to the bottom of the next tank and are _____. Finally _____ is added to the liquid to _____ it. It is then safe to _____.

More Environmentally Aware Books From ECO PUBLISHING INTERNATIONAL

Here are just a few of the books published by ECO Publishing International. The full list can be seen on our web site www.ECOpublishinginternational.com

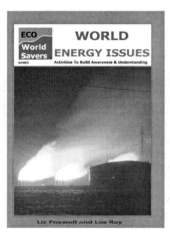

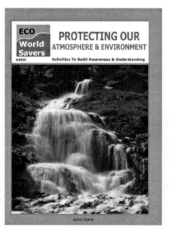